# First World War
## and Army of Occupation
# War Diary
## France, Belgium and Germany

41 DIVISION
Headquarters, Branches and Services
Royal Army Veterinary Corps
Assistant Director Veterinary Services
2 May 1916 - 31 October 1917

WO95/2624/5

The Naval & Military Press Ltd
www.nmarchive.com
Published in association with The National Archives

Published by

The Naval & Military Press Ltd

Unit 10 Ridgewood Industrial Park,

Uckfield, East Sussex,

TN22 5QE England

Tel: +44 (0) 1825 749494

www.naval-military-press.com

www.nmarchive.com

*This diary has been reprinted in facsimile from the original. Any imperfections are inevitably reproduced and the quality may fall short of modern type and cartographic standards.*

**© Crown Copyright**
**Images reproduced by permission of The National Archives, London, England, 2015.**

# Contents

| Document type | Place/Title | Date From | Date To |
|---|---|---|---|
| Heading | WO95/2624/5 | | |
| Heading | Asst Dir. Vety Services May 1916-1917 Oct 1918 Mar-1919 Sept. | | |
| Heading | War Diary For May 1916 G. P. Knott. Major. A.V.C. A.D.V.S. 41st Division Vol 1 | | |
| War Diary | Aldershot | 02/05/1916 | 02/05/1916 |
| War Diary | Havre | 03/05/1916 | 04/05/1916 |
| War Diary | Merris | 05/05/1916 | 30/05/1916 |
| Heading | War Diary For June 1916 G. P. Knott. Major. A.V.C. A.D.V.S. 41st Division Vol 2 | | |
| War Diary | Steenwerck | 02/06/1916 | 30/06/1916 |
| Heading | War Diary For July 1916 G. P. Knott Major A.V.C. A.D.V.S. 41st Division. Vol 3 | | |
| War Diary | Steenwerck | 01/07/1916 | 31/07/1916 |
| Heading | War Diary For August 1916 G.P. Knott. Major A.D.V.S. 41st Division. Vol 4 | | |
| War Diary | Steenwerck | 01/08/1916 | 17/08/1916 |
| War Diary | Fletre | 18/08/1916 | 22/08/1916 |
| War Diary | Ailly | 24/08/1916 | 31/08/1916 |
| Heading | War Diary For Sept 1916 G. P. Knott A.D.V.S. 41st Div. Vol 5 | | |
| War Diary | Ailly | 01/09/1916 | 05/09/1916 |
| War Diary | Buire Sur L'ancer | 06/09/1916 | 10/09/1916 |
| War Diary | Bellevue Farm | 11/09/1916 | 14/09/1916 |
| War Diary | Belle Vue Farm Near Albert | 14/09/1916 | 15/09/1916 |
| War Diary | Belle Vue Farm | 16/09/1916 | 18/09/1916 |
| War Diary | Ribemont | 19/09/1916 | 30/09/1916 |
| Heading | War Diary October 1916 G. P. Knott Major A.V.C. A.D.V.S. 41st Division Vol 6 | | |
| War Diary | Ribemont | 01/10/1916 | 05/10/1916 |
| War Diary | E H-Central | 06/10/1916 | 10/10/1916 |
| War Diary | Buire | 11/10/1916 | 15/10/1916 |
| War Diary | Hallencourt | 16/10/1916 | 19/10/1916 |
| War Diary | Fletre | 20/10/1916 | 22/10/1916 |
| War Diary | Renninghelst | 24/10/1916 | 30/11/1916 |
| Heading | War Diary December 1916 G.P. Knott. Major. A.D.V.S. 41st Division Vol 8 | | |
| Heading | D.H.Q (A) Herewith "War Diaries" For December 1916. A.D.V.S. D.O.C. M.V.S. | | |
| War Diary | Reninghelst | 01/12/1916 | 31/12/1916 |
| Heading | War Diary For January 1917 G. P. Knott Major A.V.C. A.D.V.S. 41st Division Vol 9 | | |
| War Diary | Reninghelst | 01/01/1917 | 31/01/1917 |
| Heading | War Diaries For February 1917 G.P. Knott. Major. A.D.V.S 41st Division And O.C. 52nd Mobile Vety Section Vol 10 | | |
| War Diary | Reninghelst | 01/02/1917 | 31/03/1917 |
| Heading | War Diaries For April 1917 G.P. Knott. Major A.D.V.S. 41st Division O.C. 52nd Mobile Veterinary Section Vol 12 | | |

| | | | |
|---|---|---|---|
| War Diary | Reninghelst | 01/04/1917 | 27/04/1917 |
| Heading | War Diaries For May 1917 G.P. Knott. Major. A.D.V.S 41st Division Vol 13 | | |
| War Diary | Reninghelst | 03/05/1917 | 30/06/1917 |
| Heading | War Diary For July 1917 C.W.B. Sikes. Major. W.C. D.A.D.V.S. 41st Division Vol 15 | | |
| War Diary | Westoutre | 01/07/1917 | 01/07/1917 |
| War Diary | Berthen | 02/07/1917 | 25/07/1917 |
| War Diary | Westoutre | 26/07/1917 | 31/07/1917 |
| Heading | War Diaries For August 1917 C.W.B. Sikes. Major A.V.C. D.A.D.V.S. 41st Division. O.C. 52nd M.V.S. 16 | | |
| War Diary | Westoutre | 01/08/1917 | 16/08/1917 |
| War Diary | Berthen | 18/08/1917 | 21/08/1917 |
| War Diary | Wizernes | 22/08/1917 | 31/08/1917 |
| Heading | War Diary For Sept 1917 C.W.B. Sikes. Major. A.V.C. D.A.D.V.S. 41st Division Vol 17 | | |
| War Diary | Wizernes | 01/09/1917 | 15/09/1917 |
| War Diary | Zevecoten | 16/09/1917 | 23/09/1917 |
| War Diary | Caistre | 24/09/1917 | 26/09/1917 |
| War Diary | La Panne | 27/09/1917 | 30/09/1917 |
| Heading | War Diaries For October 1917 C.W.B. Sikes. Major A.V.C. D.A.D.V.S. 41st Division And O.C. 52nd Mobile Veterinary Section Vol 18 | | |
| War Diary | La Panne | 02/10/1917 | 07/10/1917 |
| War Diary | St Idesbalde | 08/10/1917 | 29/10/1917 |
| War Diary | Malo Les Bains | 30/10/1917 | 31/10/1917 |

W 097/262 4(5) 96 cm

W 095/125 4(5) 60 cm

# 41ST DIVISION

FRANCE

ASST DIR. VETY SERVICES

MAY 1916 – ~~DEC 1918~~ 1917 OCT

1918 MAR — 1919 SEPT

(Less 1917 Nov — 1918 Feb in Italy)

Box FRANCE 2624

've# War Diary
### For May 1916

G.P. Knott. Major, A.V.C
A.D.V.S. 41st Division

# WAR DIARY
## or
## INTELLIGENCE SUMMARY.
*(Erase heading not required.)*

Army Form C. 2118.

| Place | Date | Hour | Summary of Events and Information | Remarks and references to Appendices |
|---|---|---|---|---|
| Aldershot | May 1st | | War Diary of A.D.V.S. 41 Division | |
| | | | Entrained with Head Quarter staff for Southampton. Left Southampton about 8-30 p.m. Arrived Havre 11 A.M. Owing the voyage had the horses & loaded. Horses taken off. Animals proved in coming off all the animals on this ship arrived but well and ready for work. Of all the other transports animals sent out M-Saddles & unharmed with the result that a number within a few days of landing were unserviceable from sore withers & saddle and girth galls. Shoeing the is any plan & its working in going out in my opinion is a mistake & should be altered. It is not the shoeing in general, the method of animal hire were | |
| Havre | May 2nd | | Entrain number animal horses were upheaved at— Havre, shortly some minor injuries | |

# WAR DIARY
## or
## INTELLIGENCE SUMMARY.
*(Erase heading not required.)*

Army Form C. 2118.

| Place | Date | Hour | Summary of Events and Information | Remarks and references to Appendices |
|---|---|---|---|---|
| Havre | May 3 | | No animals had the places on account of suffering with an injection in contagious disease - of suffering | |
| | May 4 | | Left Havre 6 P.M. | |
| | May 5 | | Arrived Rouen. | |
| Rouen | May 10 | | All units with the exception of the D.A.G. had arrived. Owing to the large number of casualties the want of picks, have had the utmost want in Div. - Several large Phoneis fly where that all Kingson stables in Rochetta by themselves and kill when once under not - have I uncertain temper. | |
| | May 18 | | Attended a Head Quarters Staff Conference under the matter Div. on which is not any of presenting the proof of the motor car which is not marked greatly but the use of the H.O.R.S. this difficulty has always existed & it is only by defying a new try we can obtain it - to carry out - the necessary work. | |

# WAR DIARY
## or
## INTELLIGENCE SUMMARY

Army Form C. 2118.

| Place | Date | Hour | Summary of Events and Information | Remarks and references to Appendices |
|---|---|---|---|---|
| Mons | May 25th | | Owing to the continuance of casualties from kicks the matter has been brought before the Principal D.G.V. who forwarded a circular letter to all O.C.S. together with a return showing the total number of casualties from preventable causes. | |
| | May 26 | | Published a divisional order stating employer horses would not be admitted to Field Pty Return | |
| | May 27th | | The Division moved to Steenwerck | |

A.D.V.S. Vol 2
41st Div.
June

# War Diary
## For June 1916

G. P. Knott. Major. A.V.C
A.D.V.S. 41st Division

# WAR DIARY
## or
## INTELLIGENCE SUMMARY.

(Erase heading not required.)

Army Form C. 2118.

Instructions regarding War Diaries and Intelligence Summaries are contained in F. S. Regs., Part II. and the Staff Manual respectively. Title pages will be prepared in manuscript.

| Place | Date | Hour | Summary of Events and Information | Remarks and references to Appendices |
|---|---|---|---|---|
| Steenwerck | June 2 | | Casualties due to kicks are becoming less owing to a large extent to the horses becoming accustomed to standing on lines tightly and ample care being taken in their management, horses rather being picketted by themselves. | |
| | June 4th | | Two cases of Mange reported in the 2 & Amy R.E. three horses and Tin which were reemed at Habe Kruploe casualties, the affected horses are being inacerated and all necessary steps taken. | |
| | June 11th | | Three crops of Mange was reported in the 127 L.Q.A. our attached Unit, these were inacerated and usual steps taken. | |
| | June 16 | | A case of Mange was found in the Head Qts D.the 189 Bde R.F.A. This horse was standing in some stables which about ten other rather away from the main party, on inspection found | |

T2134. Wt. W708—776. 500000. 4/15. Sir J. C. & S.

# WAR DIARY
## or
## INTELLIGENCE SUMMARY.
*(Erase heading not required.)*

Army Form C. 2118.

| Place | Date | Hour | Summary of Events and Information | Remarks and references to Appendices |
|---|---|---|---|---|
| Jemmal Jmeloh | | | On inspection found all the horses in a filthy condition, evidently their stables were infective and the filthy condition of the horses predisposed to infection setting in place. A great many R.A. Units are very short of men for grooming purposes, with the result I am hard put getting horses groomed. The men being called away for building gun emplacements etc. | |
| | June 18th | | Lieut Sewell A.V.C. who has been O.C. 62 Mob. Vety. Section proceeds to the Base Vety. Hospital at Calais and is replaced by Capt. Sandeman A.V.C. from the 3rd Division. | |
| | June 19th | | During the night October 16–17 June the Germans were subjected to a Gas attack. A large number of animals were affected — 406 in a very mild degree, 14 moderately and thirty severely — A Divisional order is being published | |

# WAR DIARY
## or
## INTELLIGENCE SUMMARY.
*(Erase heading not required.)*

Army Form C. 2118.

| Place | Date | Hour | Summary of Events and Information | Remarks and references to Appendices |
|---|---|---|---|---|
| Stennwich | June 17 | | Published intradual work & exercise diary not with effective times, and that anytime anything in our area which the teen fancier my matter from flight should be immediately reported to the V.O. concerned. | |
| | June 20th | | Most of the grand animals are now recovered, work and exercise resumed | |
| | June 26th | | Sent a report to the Q.O.C. 9th Dunion & the D.D.V.S. 9th & Army on the effects 9th recent gas attack. All animals event they cannot surely affected are fit to resume work in 7-10 days, touping hearing told officers the as necessary for their macaringz knowe there which were most surely affected will be kept under special observation and reported upon from time to time. | |

# WAR DIARY
## or
## INTELLIGENCE SUMMARY.
(Erase heading not required.)

Army Form C. 2118.

| Place | Date | Hour | Summary of Events and Information | Remarks and references to Appendices |
|---|---|---|---|---|
| Stewmarsh | June 24th | | Have found a case of neglect amongst the slayers of the Divisional Artillery, by they arrivals they always seem more of his [isolates] from other times I think any time [unclear] contractor to from one [little] to [little], all we are doing [unclear] healer as if affected as the [drayers] had got out on foot [unclear] [landscapes] on trouble in getting it all got — then he has been more [unscrupulous] anyhow for me, in connection with [slamming] the use of a motor car. Today I secured a circular from the D.V.S. saying [charge] to M. [Lt] moreover that A.D.V.S. are [truely] through [equivalent] inspection they also secure a [conference] from D.[haupt], saying G.S.O.'s have given instruction that motor cars are not to be met for that purpose but — however, see the A.Q.O. [etc]. O. why say the military [carrotie] require this — by matter how well we car are no mark in horse [breed] than in [unclear] that |  |

| Place | Date | Hour | Summary of Events and Information | Remarks and references to Appendices |
|---|---|---|---|---|
| Wormwood | June 27th | | that with the help of a rider we could do it — a lot better, especially were there impediments necessary when the ambulance wishes to prevent O.C.'s hunts being so much attention to whole management — no doubt would myself experience inconvenience in turn if the A.D.V.S. had the same opportunity in dealing — the use for matter which was urgently advocated for their use by the Hon. Price 20 |  |
|  | June 29th | | attended a conference at Guildhall Pharos, when the D.D.V.S. & discussed the evacuation of horses by rail when happened— rail cases are at Land France to have road— |  |
|  | June 30. | | Decided on an advanced nursing station should one be required. |  |

War Diary for July 1916
G. P. Knott Major A.V.C.
A.D.V.S. 41st Division

**WAR DIARY**
or
**INTELLIGENCE SUMMARY**
(Erase heading not required.)

Army Form C. 2118.

| Place | Date | Hour | Summary of Events and Information | Remarks and references to Appendices |
|---|---|---|---|---|
| Steenwerck | July 1st | | Inspected all animals. The H1 Divisional horses in good condition under the exception of 1 M.T. which were thin & 2 which were suffering from debility. The latter will be evacuated. The few horses & ponies drawn about had there were separate scraping at debug examined. | |
| | July 2nd | | Inspected the horses of the 18 Div R.F.A. A. Battery horses very good. D.A.C. horses attached in dirty condition. B. Battery horses not good - duty the lime seed like a wind swollen tick up the horses in a filthy condition. C. Battery horses much too that together badly want cleaning. D. Battery horses had collars went wringing and cleaning. The above animals were founded by C.R.A. 2 Div. All V.O.'s have been warned by on the outlook for mange and apart any even only suspicious cases. | |

| Place | Date | Hour | Summary of Events and Information | Remarks and references to Appendices |
|---|---|---|---|---|
| Stanwick | July 2nd | | Scanned the following Divisional order the published Horses — Owing to the prevalence of mange which frequently first attacks horses head and muzzle, head collars should be removed and inspected at least once a day and the horses head thoroughly groomed before the head collar is replaced | |
| | July 3rd | | Inspected A Echelon D.A.C. at Echo. Arranged to have the necessary ability found for the Canves Muffle. Inspected A Echelon in the Afternoon, saw a number of horses and mules which had been subject in of account of having suspicious marks on their under neath head collars, they seemed due to a large extend to the head collars hung rather tight, Nothing beyond a few slight sign of all being washed or mud. Maps in use for the new camp— | |

# WAR DIARY
## or
## INTELLIGENCE SUMMARY.
(Erase heading not required.)

Army Form C. 2118.

| Place | Date | Hour | Summary of Events and Information | Remarks and references to Appendices |
|---|---|---|---|---|
| Stennwick | June 4th | | Inspected the 183rd Bde R.F.A. and forwarded the following notes to the C.R.A. 41 Divnp. — | |
| | | | A Battery — Horses look well but there are too many in the light-red. | |
| | | | B " Condition good on the whole but badly turned and grooming. | |
| | | | C " Horses first rate but their heels are clipped far too closely which means lead to cracked heels. | |
| | | | D " Horses wing good. — | |
| | | | The leather hand of the eye fringes are too short and in many cases have tied up the horses getting them attached. Do not tye the ears. — Have informed D.A.D.S. — | |
| | July 5th | | Inspected D. Battery 189th Bde R.F.A. when a case of Sarcoptic Mange had been demonstrated. Picture up three I have keeping taken the isolate of line the ill marked. — | |

**Army Form C. 2118.**

# WAR DIARY
## or
## INTELLIGENCE SUMMARY.
*(Erase heading not required.)*

| Place | Date | Hour | Summary of Events and Information | Remarks and references to Appendices |
|---|---|---|---|---|
| Stenwerk | July 6 | | Inspected the 190th R.F.A. – | |
| | | | A. Battery – Horses fair, too many thin ones. – | |
| | | | B. Battery – good " | |
| | | | C. Battery – " " | |
| | | | D. Battery – good. – | |
| | | | 228 Coy R.E. Horses in poor condition, two reported as suspence of having mange. Also four contacts – | |
| | | | 237th R.E. Horses from all race of Meuse | |
| | | | 233d – good – | |

# WAR DIARY
## or
## INTELLIGENCE SUMMARY.
*(Erase heading not required.)*

Army Form C. 2118.

| Place | Date | Hour | Summary of Events and Information | Remarks and references to Appendices |
|---|---|---|---|---|
| Stamwick | July 7th | | Inspected D Battery 189th Bde R.F.A. where two cases of Lacache Ongue Land recently been detected - picked out one horse which one file kept separate & under observation - | |
| | | | Sent the first batch horses to Etaples for inoculation by barge. I was unable to go myself as was very short of a car. Car was unavailable could not afford the time which would be needed if that wilt still stands - | |
| | July | 8th | Inspected the rest of 189th Bde R.F.A from - A Battery - Condition Unknown from - B Battery - Horses in very dirty condition today the lines, fresh manure is being placed in old manure heaps. C Battery - Condition from - D Battery, Condition known from - as very mange land been detected in this battery, the but supervision possible is required - | |

Army Form C. 2118.

# WAR DIARY
## or
## INTELLIGENCE SUMMARY.
*(Erase heading not required.)*

Instructions regarding War Diaries and Intelligence Summaries are contained in F.S. Regs., Part II. and the Staff Manual respectively. Title pages will be prepared in manuscript.

| Place | Date | Hour | Summary of Events and Information | Remarks and references to Appendices |
|---|---|---|---|---|
| Shorncliffe | July 3rd | | D.D.V.S. inspected 2nd Mobile Vety Section. Paid special attention to condition of horses high were apparently recovering rapidly with the exception of two that were affected only on the head and neck. The legs from the injection appear from the tracks that are left in the standing when thundermade. | |
| | July 4th | | Office work in the morning. In the afternoon went to Etchinghill Rifle Range which is used to exercise horses. | |
| | July 10th | | Inspected D. Battery 189 R.F.A. No sick cases of mange. Horses appear well. Having more frequency of case generally. In the afternoon inspected 52 Mule Vety Section. | |
| | July 11th | | Inspected the A. & B. Coys. R.E. Five horses are being clipped & washed in Malabet, having been contacts of the mange cases. | |

T2134. Wt. W708-776. 500000. 4/15. Sir J.C. & S.

# WAR DIARY
## or
## INTELLIGENCE SUMMARY.
*(Erase heading not required.)*

Army Form C. 2118.

Instructions regarding War Diaries and Intelligence Summaries are contained in F. S. Regs., Part II. and the Staff Manual respectively. Title pages will be prepared in manuscript.

| Place | Date | Hour | Summary of Events and Information | Remarks and references to Appendices |
|---|---|---|---|---|
| Stanmich | July 12 | | Inspector road its agent of the 124th Brigade R.F.A. In the afternoon the Head Qrs of No 2. Pontoon Park R.E. | |
| | July 13 | | 2nd Lieut Walker went to late in the lecture Room the D.A.C. | |
| | July 14 | | Visited 5 & 6 inch section in the morning. 2.30 p.m. Conference V.O.S. 27th Division. | |
| | July 15 | | Visited Mule Pit Section. A considerable number of animals have to be evacuated from time to time suffering with Debility, the great majority being animals of a certain type that is heart rather, having ratted one rachis, feeble headed mules, weighing in age from 10 to 20 yrs old, animals in fact, that should never have been purchased – a large percentage of the mefficiency of Army animals | |

| Place | Date | Hour | Summary of Events and Information | Remarks and references to Appendices |
|---|---|---|---|---|
| Ommich | July 13th | — | is in my opinion due indirectly to much to faulty information | |
| | July 14th | | Enter enemy 17th Reinforts of the 12.3 Inf: Regt. Prince of the lines which had retired from East-Iront as the one was much impaired, they are very type advanced in yesterday. They suffered very large losses, advancing yesterday. 4 our 17 Btn were cooking lunch short-handed fully at Say 6-6 pm 12 — Some Othrun wheel, night Line seen during the S.A. & one obm. Round the army again — | |
| | July 14th | | I have had to send the following telegram to the 1.C. & Echln D.A.C. — Regt cannot engage — today motor not available with the present system there is little advantage in making attempts before fuel, as one may be informed at any time that the Omnifirt Coy is not available | |

# WAR DIARY
## or
## INTELLIGENCE SUMMARY.
(Erase heading not required.)

**Army Form C. 2118.**

| Place | Date | Hour | Summary of Events and Information | Remarks and references to Appendices |
|---|---|---|---|---|
| Stonewich | July 17 | | On the other hand I am afraid has not been made an A.D.V.S. very find [illegible] mustering a unit many the animals out, his Officer [illegible] says he cannot always get into touch with Reg O.C. to meet him due to things no when mornings the unit [illegible] the time very unfit. He been almost wasted — If his informed at the [illegible] moment that a car is not available, it also means a morning since a bus ago to as he cannot then made the necessary arrangements — This [illegible] frequently occurs — | |
| | | | [illegible] the Machine Gun Companies of the 122-123-124 Inf Bde the placing the mules was in a Magazine state — Each Coy has no re S-S. onto the coy, it seems so anthriny Reported the matter to D-H.Q. — | |

Army Form C. 2118.

# WAR DIARY
## or
## INTELLIGENCE SUMMARY.
(Erase heading not required.)

Instructions regarding War Diaries and Intelligence Summaries are contained in F. S. Regs., Part II. and the Staff Manual respectively. Title pages will be prepared in manuscript.

| Place | Date | Hour | Summary of Events and Information | Remarks and references to Appendices |
|---|---|---|---|---|
| Stenwork | 18th July | | Inspected 140 Field Ambulance. Found all animals in good working condition. | |
| | 20th | | Inspected the D.A.C. at Leche. a note-horse available. Horses all in fair condition with the exception of 32. The Horse Certificate recommending in name of Linseed. | |
| | 21st | | Visited Mule Section in the morning. In the afternoon had the weekly Conference of Divisional V.O.S. | |
| | 23rd | | Inspected 105 Remounts at Italin. Gave a certificate to A.D.R. Logging two eye sufferers. Fleine officially sent large a fairly good batch, had on arrival maintaining some left the try lacked fat. | |

**WAR DIARY**
or
~~INTELLIGENCE SUMMARY.~~
*(Erase heading not required.)*

Army Form C. 2118.

19

| Place | Date | Hour | Summary of Events and Information | Remarks and references to Appendices |
|---|---|---|---|---|
| Denmark | July 25th | | Inspected the 328 Coy. Mks R.E. Sir knew no reply to Enquiries re France — but the inexperienced mannerism was partly to blame. Demonstrates the Recruits — Inspection arrival of the 13th Field Ambulance. All working well. No reply as to hat & rifle fill — afternoon counted the M.V.S.B. | |
| | July 26th | | Inspected 150. Field Ambulance. All arrived in good condition with practically no kick — | |
| | July 28th | | Usual Conference of Divisional Returning Officers — | |
| | July 30th | | Inspected 6.2 Inch Pdr. Section | |
| | July 31st | | Visited the D.O.V.S. 2d Army — in order to discuss the subject of Divisional Horse baths, as a means of preventing the spread of mange.    Sd Robert Sharer A.V.V.S. | |

T2134. Wt. W708—776. 500000. 4/15. Sir J.C.&S.

Vol 4

War Diary
for August 1916

G. P. Knott. Major.
A.D.V.S. 41st Division.

# WAR DIARY
## or
## INTELLIGENCE SUMMARY.
*(Erase heading not required.)*

Army Form C. 2118.

| Place | Date | Hour | Summary of Events and Information | Remarks and references to Appendices |
|---|---|---|---|---|
| Bkmmmrck | August 1st | | Visited No. 10-12-9-13 Base Vety Hospitals in order to see the arrangements & the difficulties met in the treatment of mange. | |
| | 2nd | | Saw plays for & inspected hay bath & industry demo Vby B.O.C. through the C.R.E. Walked the matter over with the D.D.V.S. of Army, who took away duplicate plans &c. | |
| | 3rd | | Inspected the D managed train — all the horses were in good condition — there appeared to be suffering with mange. | |
| | 4th | | Inspected 187th Btte R.F.A. A 187 – very good. B – fair. D 187. Too many thin horses — Army Inspector 187 – these good. An unproved stable management — no case of mange. | |

# WAR DIARY
## or
## INTELLIGENCE SUMMARY
(Erase heading not required.)

Army Form C. 2118.

| Place | Date | Hour | Summary of Events and Information | Remarks and references to Appendices |
|---|---|---|---|---|
| Steenwerck | August 4, | | Inspected the 21 Signal Coy. Horses & mules in most excellent condition. | |
| | | | 123 Bde. M.M. — { 123rd. Inf. Coy. Annual very good. 20th D.L.I. very many thin horses. condition poor - 2 horse hipped 10th R.W.R. very good. 11th R.W.S. In among thin horses. condition poor. 23rd Middlesex - Improvement in last month. | |
| | | 6th | Inspected the 183 Bde. R.F.A. — A Batt. horses good. B Batt. much improved since inspection a month ago. C Batt - horses good. D Batt. very good with the exception of five thin ones. | |
| | | 6th | Inspected the 122 & 124 machine gun companies. Signals & both units in very fair condition particularly the 124th. | |

| Place | Date | Hour | Summary of Events and Information | Remarks and references to Appendices |
|---|---|---|---|---|
| Steenwerck | July 1st | | Inspected a detachment of the 2nd Canadian Reserve Park — Found 16 cases of mange. Some in a fairly advanced state. There had been an inopportune lapse between the attachment, and another seven apparently hygiene contacts were being evacuated. Horses along with which were subsequent detachments. He declared free of mange — This matter has been spoken to the 2nd Army — Spoke to the D.D.V.S. 2nd Army. | |
| | 4th | | Finished 5-9 mule Vety Return | |
| | 5th | | Spent the month of the 12th & 12A Infantry Brigade with the object of seeing all weak horses & mules that would not be fit for hard work in fourteen days time. With the exception of a very few found all in good condition. | |

# WAR DIARY

| Place | Date | Hour | Summary of Events and Information |
|---|---|---|---|
| Steenwerck | August 9 | | Inspected the 228 - 233 - 237 R.E. Field Coys. - The 228 & 233 Coys. were working with 4 Divn. They had very little thought to give this, but Coy 237 were helping 2nd thougth to give this, first Coy has had a lot of moving about - and may accept their conduct & their Lack of condition - under the GOC to form in thin line to become chaps of private but those in bad condition - |
| | | | 190th Bde R.F.A. - all horses in fair condition, why Major the acted I want I know - appeared stained - which I am told carefully he helped owing to many men being taken away both for leave & recruits - Practically all the R.A. horses in our Division are suffering more or less during the same cause |

# WAR DIARY
## or
## INTELLIGENCE SUMMARY.
(Erase heading not required.)

Army Form C. 2118.

| Place | Date | Hour | Summary of Events and Information | Remarks and references to Appendices |
|---|---|---|---|---|
| Steenwerck | August 10 | | Capt Likes A.V.C was reporting by the O.C. D.T. to be ill. No medical report received. Visited an urgent case in the line. Inspection of the 189 Bde R.F.A. — all looking fairly well, very few weaknesses. Casting. D.A.C. B acelym - all reporting well. D.A.C. A acelym - No 2 section travelling new horses to inoculate with serum suffering with Debility all use thy by horses, hadn't healed rapidly that are almost unfit to stay in condition & unfed. A couple of Mayors of mine & two the same class use in bad condition. | |
| | August 11 | | Conference of Veterinary Officers of the Division. | |
| | August 12 | | Attended a Conference of A.D.V.S at Bailleul under the D.D.V.S. of 2nd Army | |

# WAR DIARY
## INTELLIGENCE SUMMARY
*(Erase heading not required.)*

Army Form C. 2118.

| Place | Date | Hour | Summary of Events and Information | Remarks and references to Appendices |
|---|---|---|---|---|
| Stormonth | August 10th | | Visited 5.2 Amb Fd Sectn. Inspected the method of laying hares together that he intended use if they were eight - may 2 Caprof worth of times to Samrt Druse to the Reenns Returning hospital — | |
| | 14th | | Inspected 138 Field Ambulance arranged for afternoon then Inspected the O D V S to he 10 a.m. f 9th & 23 Divn. Called in the afternoon arranged the lectures on of Ind Sectn Multile S/C | |
| | 15th | | Visited all R. of Mayon true with the D.D.R. 2 lying he who very pleased with the condition of gass masks — | |
| | 18th | | Visited 5 Druck Rty Lectures — | |
| | 19th | | Proceeded by Car to Flake | |

# WAR DIARY
## or
## INTELLIGENCE SUMMARY.
(Erase heading not required.)

Army Form C. 2118.

| Place | Date | Hour | Summary of Events and Information | Remarks and references to Appendices |
|---|---|---|---|---|
| Flête | August 1915 | | Visited the 123 Bde Head Qts. No Casualties reported on march. | |
| | 21st | | Visited Military Police & Royal Engi: No Casualties- Inspected post Remounts- not a bad lot- | |
| | 22nd | | Left Steenwerck for Ailly Le Haut Clocher- with the A.A.O.M.G. - D.A.D.O.S. in a motor- | |
| Ailly- | 24th | | Met Sir John Dunun arrived at in the train- | |
| | 25th | | Visited the 124 & 122 Inf: Brigades | |
| | 26th | | Conference D.F.O.S. Arranged Ambulance Pranh- | |
| | 28, | | Visited Mobile Vety Section & some other R.A. Units- | |

## WAR DIARY
### INTELLIGENCE SUMMARY

**Army Form C. 2118.**

| Place | Date | Hour | Summary of Events and Information | Remarks and references to Appendices |
|---|---|---|---|---|
| Celly | Aug 30 | | Visits 19th Middlesex — During fs. reconnd. rain it was almost impossible to see the lines, which in some cases was standing up to their fetlocks in mud. Visit neg[illegible] from Service Bay Ent. — ng no serious case of casualties. | |
| | Aug 31st | | Visits the Signal Coy. R.E. also 52 Ind. Vet. Section in the town found two impressive cases of mange. Several dips being taken. | |

G.P. [illegible signature]
A.V.C.
211 [illegible]

vol 5

War Diary
for Sept 1916
G.P. Knott A.D.V.S. 11th Div

# WAR DIARY
## INTELLIGENCE SUMMARY

**Army Form C. 2118**

28

| Place | Date | Hour | Summary of Events and Information | Remarks and references to Appendices |
|---|---|---|---|---|
| Billy | 1/9/16 | | Conference of Divisional V.O.S. Gave instructions that Reg. receipts from the O.C. Mob. Vet. Section are told fwd to O.C. Divnl S of J. in a case of urgency a letter (with effect) should but sent to the O.C. Mob Section when the horse is admitted. The V.O. of the Corps Unit is responsible for this. | |
| | 2nd | | Inspected some 9th Hampshire — The 123rd Brigade — a horse of the 123 machine gun Cy had died of Colic — Ing Stud Officer had enquired but no warm dressing for this. Divisional horse shoer, Capt Duncan ill — | |
| | 3rd | | | |
| | 4 | | Inspected 52 Mob Vet. Inspection Unit a great syphilis — they were leave for to the unit from Captn Russ — Capt Dudgeon complaining that they were well — Sgt Allan Metcalf dismounted. D.C. recommended vaccination — | |

# WAR DIARY
## or
## INTELLIGENCE SUMMARY.
(Erase heading not required.)

Army Form C. 2118.

| Place | Date | Hour | Summary of Events and Information | Remarks and references to Appendices |
|---|---|---|---|---|
| Rully | 5th | | Arranged with the D.V.S. for Capt Perry to relieve Capt Liles in Veterinary charge of the Divisional train. Capt Liles relieved Capt Andrews in Command of the M.V.S. Capt Andrews in Veterinary Charge Deck. I regret this officer leaving the Division. | |
| Briere Ambagnes | 6th | | Interviewed me with the AA & QMG & DADVS. Spent the afternoon interviewing found posting of the different Collecting posts when the Units are to be. | |
| | 7th | | Visited the 122 & 124 Infantry Brigades - the DTC & M.V.S. | |
| | 8th | | Conference of Veterinary Officers - wishing it unusual new instructions to O.C. Units to see that horses are properly lay up. Owing to horses staying & eating wheat Drought cases of Colic have occurred. | |

Army Form C. 2118.

# WAR DIARY
## or
## INTELLIGENCE SUMMARY.
(Erase heading not required.)

| Place | Date | Hour | Summary of Events and Information | Remarks and references to Appendices |
|---|---|---|---|---|
| Bruay Sur l'Ouene | Sept 9th | 9 a.m. | Received a visit from the D.D.V.S. 4th Army. He inspected the M.V.S. In the afternoon inspected all the Company of the R.E. of the 19th Middlesex. The R.E. horses are in fair condition but on the light side. Sent 5 from 237 Coy, 3 from 233 Coy & 1 Both 22t Coy to M.V.S. for recuperative purposes with debility. No animals found affected with mange. | |
| | | 10 - | Inspected 1 & 2 B/s R.F.A. horses getting a lot thin owing to extra work & hot weather. Interviewed G.O.C. Division suggested all horses should be walked if possible from troughs daily. be kept in each line when time allows. Efforts & care special attention Chaff & hand cut if necessary. The watering four times daily. the chaff & rubing in case of thin horses is essential. G.O.C agreed & will take steps to see it carried out. | |

# WAR DIARY
## INTELLIGENCE SUMMARY

Army Form C. 2118.

| Place | Date | Hour | Summary of Events and Information | Remarks and references to Appendices |
|---|---|---|---|---|
| Pall Mall Farm | Sept 11th | 11" | Inspected the 18th Brigade R.F.A. Horses in fair condition in the whole, though commencing in some cases before the saddles & had meats. Should add Off's & M.V.S. to drive to Albert. | |
| | 13th | | Inspected the 190th Bde R.F.A. Horses in fair condition, up to opinion the unit by slightly made, was near the front to draw the wants of the hard work. | |
| | 17th | | Inspected the 3rd Regt 7th mule teams was under to permanent road for sufficiency Transport Corps Hospital at Hamel— | |
| | 18th | | Inspected Remounts a fair lot — also the M.V.S. & the veterinary Police linen. | |

# WAR DIARY
## or
## INTELLIGENCE SUMMARY.
(Erase heading not required.)

Army Form C. 2118.

| Place | Date | Hour | Summary of Events and Information | Remarks and references to Appendices |
|---|---|---|---|---|
| Salle Sur Som | Sept 14th | | In the morning attended a Conference with the A.D's.s. of the New Zealand Division at Omaraval. In this District a Divisional Cdn. not being available the subject upon discussion was as to why that no F.S.O. had been sent from the Base to the D.D.V.S. of Army. There seem no doubt should he kept but a Central M.V.S. be called by D.D. M.V.S. fact as embracting parties as regards - (normally I think this is no doubt that we should have a Central Clearing Station run by an Officer during a big Offensive. In the afternoon I went placed a forward Watering Station in connection with the New Zealand Division. Conveying I am by C.O. From order there men are being utilised each evening out. by whom they have been any sick horses that well- away have been collected during the day. | |
| | 15. | | Milder advanced Station - no Cases had been received. Lymph Receiver units of Horses injured Shrapnel with Metal M.V.S. Lymph cleaning daily in order to be ready to move at short notice. | |

| Place | Date | Hour | Summary of Events and Information | Remarks and references to Appendices |
|---|---|---|---|---|
| Rollencourt Farm | 16th Sept | | Sirka advanced collecting station - only two Carts had been received. | |
| | 17th | | Need 4 to 6 more. Went to Pulmont in Rest area - with Infantry Brigade Divisional Horsem & Mule Vety Section - Divisional Artillery unmailed in the Line. - Local arrangements for the incoming Mule Vety Section to evacuate cases occurring in R.A. Horses. On the way to Pulmont. Latinham a Conference under the D.D.V.S. 4th Army at which it was decided to form a Casualty Clearing Station for all forward divisions at Meaulte. Districts supplying 2 Mares each of their visits were in this line the scene of only their Artillery were left in - the heavy Artry C.C. Styhen who made up with 5 H.C. There form with there mob Capt Dolittle who two men from the Section the whole to be attached to No 26 Mob Section. Capt Daniels division at Meaulte V- Hospital from a great inconvenience to A.D.V.S. My Section took over the Welbury at Pulmont from the Section pth 53 Divm. | |

| Place | Date | Hour | Summary of Events and Information | Remarks and references to Appendices |
|---|---|---|---|---|
| Rubempré | 19th Sept 16 | | I was ordered to hand a Drumraised Car mudis the 122 & 124th Infantry Brigades myself the flag of asking debilitated horses which Canadian from the extreme hard work & recent inclement weather there would be a number however I was greatly surprised only finding 11 necessary in all. I said about the annual for veterinary Careers - When visiting the Rationing Rty I find out of a large number of Casualties found to dying as the Ry Staff in an indeavor to shew when within strict fortnight they had seen numbers were improved. We complete ten Casualties had occurred I am at a loss to understand their indent to a number of horses they did not care not requested. Putting the hard facts of things the occurred in this Division in it & with being exhibited the R.A. multiple horse Manages. I am answering have my doubts — | 124th |

# WAR DIARY
## INTELLIGENCE SUMMARY
*(Erase heading not required.)*

Army Form C. 2118.

| Place | Date | Hour | Summary of Events and Information | Remarks and references to Appendices |
|---|---|---|---|---|
| Edmonk | 19/9/16 | | Office work & M.V.S. in the morning. Captain inspected the horses of the Divisional Train and made all arrangements the condition generally. Evacuated two for debility – one for chronic laminitis. | |
| | 20/9/16 | | Saw Lieut. Long A.S.C. who replaced Lt. Milner under Dormant-Inefficiency. Inspected Horses of 15 Cty & arranged inspection of horses by vets of D.D.V.S Litany. | |
| | 21/9/16 | | Visited the lines of the Heavy Art. Rd & two of the Wagons was very owing to the head of the Batty not having informed him of proposed visit as they had told him would. | |
| | 22/9/16 | | Inspected the horses of the D.A.C. 189 Bde R.F.A. Two batteries 190 Bde R.F.A. In consequence furnished a | |

| Place | Date | Hour | Summary of Events and Information | Remarks and references to Appendices |
|---|---|---|---|---|
| Warwick | 23/9/16 | | Went thg G.O.C. Remm. states that horses came to Jehutstalen lines & layer under the care of the men is becoming deplorable. This Condition is attributed to the hard work & bad health they had recently been exposed to and insufficient food & irregular times of feeding — Recommends an extra feed of meals, oats 2 lbs & hay 2 lbs to 2.5 p of the light-draught horses for the period f no duty [?]. No mule found — thinks the lady made horses which should be most — Most these should be a flying scale of feed. Cavalry horses — a horse that be given too much accepting First wont refuse it him — Give French hay & 12 pods to get ready horses for R.D. horses if really watched had the two the hay which is to be made up locally. If some cannot be obtained then it is not-required. Given the full chaves from Remts. Very heavy had to dntm men suffm with collins, forty age — the reason now is producing meaduon what the Cavalier is ? | |

**Army Form C. 2118.**

# WAR DIARY
## or
## INTELLIGENCE SUMMARY.
*(Erase heading not required.)*

| Place | Date | Hour | Summary of Events and Information | Remarks and references to Appendices |
|---|---|---|---|---|
| Ribemont | 28/9/16 | | Visited the ADvS 56th Division — in reference to check with him the evacuation of R.A. horses. Divn. Surreon. During into large number of debility cases that have recently occurred. I again advised a report to the G.O.C., R.A. should he inform + not informed before that the P.S.C. R.A. should he informed + nothing effective re stable management, feeding out — till they note were misprerent. At the meeting arrangements in need of improvemt. — | |
| | 29/9/16 | | Moved my mobile vty Section 15 vans hearwts when it would be more convenient for evacuations from the B.A. & R.E. Inspected the horses of Capt. Lee late Lieut Murgoah's Corps howitz + Pk Stores all of the mobile Section for mention in despatches | |
| | 30/9/16 | | Visited mobile Section — a large number of cases of shrapnel wounds are occurring. | |

R O H mgf mayor
A D V S
41 Division

Vol 6

War Diary
October 1916
G.P. Knott Major A.V.C
A.D.V.S. 41st Division

# WAR DIARY

## or

## INTELLIGENCE SUMMARY.

(Erase heading not required.)

Army Form C. 2118.

| Place | Date | Hour | Summary of Events and Information | Remarks and references to Appendices |
|---|---|---|---|---|
| Rheims | 1/10/16 | | Visited R.A. lines in order to see the V.p.c attaching with reference to a complaint from the A.D.V.S. 65th nunn. that our ArtilLery was being sent to his M.V.S. in a very dirty state not properly cleaned. | |
| | 2-10-16 | | Sunday. 6-2 Ind Bedeion at reinforcement camp Marneffe. 9 days march 9 cases from General Dennis not being received. | |
| | 3-10-16 | | Fancy Cap Month was interviewed by the Q.M.G. with reference to his application to a Commissioned. | |
| | 4-10-16 | | Head Qrs changed to E 11- Central. G Branch & Friend Chatean. | |
| | 5-10-16 | | Inspected the three Field Companies of R.E. hinds in the whole workshop with. | |

29.

| Place | Date | Hour | Summary of Events and Information | Remarks and references to Appendices |
|---|---|---|---|---|
| E11 Central | 6-10-16 | | Went weekly conference of Veterinary Officers of the Brigade R.F.A. at no attached to this Division for veterinary in my A.D.V.S. | |
| | 7. | | Inspected the 190th Bde R.F.A.<br>A - Battery Horses fairly good.<br>B.  "    "    "   good.<br>C.  "    "    "   good.<br>D.  "    "    "   no good - many thin & debilitated horses they look as if they were not getting the care that is provided under considering all the adverse circumstances. The Artillery Stable management in a large number of cases appears to have been from indifferent training of men. Veterinary Officers of any experience are left in the majority of units which are very few Officers now by A.C.O.S. | |

Army Form C. 2118.

WAR DIARY
OR
INTELLIGENCE SUMMARY.
(Erase heading not required.)

**WAR DIARY**
or
**INTELLIGENCE SUMMARY.**
(Erase heading not required.)

Army Form C. 2118.

Instructions regarding War Diaries and Intelligence Summaries are contained in F.S. Regs., Part II. and the Staff Manual respectively. Title pages will be prepared in manuscript.

| Place | Date | Hour | Summary of Events and Information | Remarks and references to Appendices |
|---|---|---|---|---|
| F H Cantine | 8th | | Visited M.V.S. | |
| | 9th | | Inspection of Personnel of N.Z. R.A. Horses in much better condition when as a while there was a little of the strong summer air. They almost have an officer in the length twice — he about 4 very often & finally this officer will know nothing about his trouble. He is put twice for a few days & is seen by the M.O. | |
| | | 10– | Received a count from the D.D.V.S. in relation to evacuation of horses. Brought to this notice & ordered the following points — (1) Invalids of flying officers & horses (2) Some setting up there horses hastily during attacks in traffic, so sitting men on wagons had going up hill. (3) Horse transport (included) hung rigged & gun wheels off the road during bad weather. (4) The necessity of conflicting rigidly the insurance of the officers' carriages in limits adopt by the stable & by of him transport. | |

T2134. Wt. W708—776. 500000. 4/15. Sir J.C. & 8.

# WAR DIARY
## or
## INTELLIGENCE SUMMARY.
(Erase heading not required.)

Army Form C. 2118.

| Place | Date | Hour | Summary of Events and Information | Remarks and references to Appendices |
|---|---|---|---|---|
| Buire | 11th | | Head Qrs. moved back to Buire. Reported to D.H.Q.(Q) that the watering arrangements in the Franvillers Valley are inadequate. Reported to D.D.V.S. as the state of horses being received by the 52 M.V.S. | |
| | 12th | | Inspection all the R.A. with the object of ascertaining all sick list cases. Visited 2/2 Bde. ammunition T & the Ammpk. Busied with Ames the inspection when Remts. are received. Reported that the matter of watering horses forwarded as that there is no doubt that lack of sufficient water is the recurring trouble & cause of debility. | |
| | 14th | | Inspection all three (other) Infant. Troops. Inoculated 28 Ames for Venom — Various — attempt re, supply with Remounts. | |
| | 15th | | M.V.S. moved from Baou-Naux to Buire. | |

# WAR DIARY
## or
## INTELLIGENCE SUMMARY.
*(Erase heading not required.)*

Army Form C. 2118.

| Place | Date | Hour | Summary of Events and Information | Remarks and references to Appendices |
|---|---|---|---|---|
| Hallencourt | 16th Feb | | Head Qrs moved to Hallencourt. — M.V.S. moved by road to Longpré. | |
| | 18th | | Visited & insp: the M.V.S. but owing to it being too wet away & no Drummond Cars being available was unable to do so. | |
| | 19th | | Division moved to Flêtre | |
| Flêtre | 20 | | Went to Rémy fields to meet the A.D.V.S. 17th outgoing Division. Our Mobile arrived at Flêtre. Visited the 12 Div Transport. | |
| | 21 | | | |
| | 22 | | Visited Rémy fields & inspected the system 17th M.V.S. Also found system Sand site, & all can be improved. | |

# WAR DIARY
## or
## INTELLIGENCE SUMMARY.

Army Form C. 2118.

| Place | Date | Hour | Summary of Events and Information | Remarks and references to Appendices |
|---|---|---|---|---|
| Remy Siblet | Oct 24th | | Head Qrs moved to Rumplelot. | |
| | 25th | | Visited M.V.C. Handed over duties to Cpl. Edey a.v.c. as proceeding on leave in the morning. Date 26th inst. | |

44

ADYS

ADVS 4/72

Vol 7

**WAR DIARY**
or
**INTELLIGENCE SUMMARY**

Army Form C. 2118.

| Place | Date | Hour | Summary of Events and Information | Remarks and references to Appendices |
|---|---|---|---|---|
| Renningfeld | Mar 4th | | Returned early from leave. — | |
| " | 5th | | Visited M.V.S. with Asst Adj Commandant for the purpose of deciding what new buildings were required. Also inspected Mounted Infantry Transport lines & water troughs in the process of erection. — | |
| | 6th | | Receiving a wire from the D.O.V.S. 2nd Army informing me I was to act for him from the 9th to the 19th March he was about to go on leave. — | |

# WAR DIARY
## or
## INTELLIGENCE SUMMARY.
*(Erase heading not required.)*

Army Form C. 2118.

45

| Place | Date | Hour | Summary of Events and Information | Remarks and references to Appendices |
|---|---|---|---|---|
| Ronville | 19th | | Returned to Ronville from acting for the D.D.V.S. 2nd Army. | |
| | 20th | | Visited 52 Mob. Vety. Section. | |
| | 21st | | Inspected the 228, 233 + 237 Coys. R.E. All horses in very fair condition. Picketing was fair but the exercise was in a very bad state. | |
| | 23rd | | Inspected the team at Unparkreich leaving for the base with 199 debilitated horses of the R.A. | |
| | 24th | | Inspected the 13 E Field Ambulance - horses good. | |
| | | | Visited M.V.S. in the morning. Afternoon had the usual weekly conference. | |

# WAR DIARY
## or
## INTELLIGENCE SUMMARY.

*(Erase heading not required.)*

Army Form C. 2118.

| Place | Date | Hour | Summary of Events and Information | Remarks and references to Appendices |
|---|---|---|---|---|
| Romfilal- | 26 Sept | | Arranged with D-mrad. Supply Officer for an issue of nut Cake & het into Supply Officer the steam- | |
| | 27- | | Visited the Farm Major & has arranged for a supply of bricks for the M.V.S. Stable | |
| | 28- | | Visited Head Qrs. 124 by Brigade re inspection of all the transport | |
| | 29. | | D.D.V.S. 9th Army, inspected the 197, 8, 187 Bdes R.F.A. Lieut Jenner A.V.C. reported for duty vice Capt Whitham posted to 167 Bde R.F.A. | |
| | 30, | | Inspected Baggage horses in various units. Such had been put into the Stables found them subjected when put-through. Some have encountered wt. Q south H.D- by the latter the train states men turn in sickness worn out. other getting of place | |

Vol 8

War Diary
December 1916

G. P. Knott. Major.
A.D.V.S. 41st Division

**HEADQUARTERS,
A.D.V.S.,
41ST DIVISION,**
Jan 1st 1917

D.H.Q (A)

Herewith "War
Diaries" for December
1916. A.D.V.S. & O.C. M.V.S.

[signature]

MAJOR, A.V.C.,
A.D.V.S.,
41st DIVISION.

# WAR DIARY

**Army Form C. 2118.**

477

| Place | Date | Hour | Summary of Events and Information | Remarks and references to Appendices |
|---|---|---|---|---|
| Remy field | Dec 1st/16 | | D.D.V.S. 2nd Army inspected the S.A.C. & 109th Bde R.F.A. He was informed that the lines were improving but there was still a number that would eventually have to be evacuated. | |
| | 2 & 2) | | Inspected 14th Royal Hunts Regt Transport when their cases of suspected mange had been reported. Found three other suspicious cases. The three suspect cases were sent to M.V.S. Nos. 2 & 3 with orders for M.V.S. Nos. 2 & 3 on examining, given to Major Mulvick, going with supplies with Remonts. | |
| | Dec 3 | | Sarcoptic mange demonstration in cases of 11th R.W. Kents in M.V.S. informed Police & also Mulvick to ensure the suspects cases to M.V.S. Sent word that all horses of Kents were to be clipped out & immediately washed with Cryseum Sulphide. | |

# WAR DIARY
## or
## INTELLIGENCE SUMMARY.
(Erase heading not required.)

Army Form C. 2118.

| Place | Date | Hour | Summary of Events and Information | Remarks and references to Appendices |
|---|---|---|---|---|
| Rennyfield | Dec 4th | | Inspected the Emma team, all horses looked very well except the head 2 to Company which had been kept in the lower lines. One if my best ponies they were not nearly debilitated as the Bk. A. ponies due no doubt to fighting wire-end & less work but also due to better supervision & horse management. | |
| | Dec 5th | | Inspected S.2 mt reg between Velos D.A.C. trigger lines | |
| | Dec 6th | | Conference R.V-03 Mr Dunn - in the way shutted 2 Conference at Head Qts of 23rd Divisn | |
| | Dec 7 | | Inspected all the transports of the 124th Bde & Infantry Oth Avenue in the while looking well — | |

# WAR DIARY
## *or*
## INTELLIGENCE SUMMARY.
*(Erase heading not required.)*

Army Form C. 2118.

| Place | Date | Hour | Summary of Events and Information | Remarks and references to Appendices |
|---|---|---|---|---|
| Reninghelst | Dec 8th | | Visited M.V.S. in the morning. Afternoon naval conference of V.O.S. took in 204 Remounts from the D.O.R. at Hopoudrick Kuhn | |
| | | 9th | No Divisional Conference | |
| | | 10th | Inspected all animals of the Belgian Artillery — all looking extremely well. Noted few the necessity for drawing rations, two cases of lymphitic menge | |
| | | 11th | Inspected shoeing of D.T. Who regiments are being carried out by Smiths in plates. Seems the horses thirst of my Divisional Trifles up nightly. Plates had cannot furnish in one case owing to pneumonia. I'm plates on hind quarts very ugly. Irregulars in shoe depôt available in reserve. Light — Draught only. Replacement with van plates from M. Look in 200 Remts from D.D.R. at Hopoudrich Station. | |

**Army Form C. 2118.**

# WAR DIARY
## or
## ~~INTELLIGENCE SUMMARY~~
*(Erase heading not required.)*

Instructions regarding War Diaries and Intelligence Summaries are contained in F.S. Regs., Part II. and the Staff Manual respectively. Title pages will be prepared in manuscript.

| Place | Date | Hour | Summary of Events and Information | Remarks and references to Appendices |
|---|---|---|---|---|
| Remy field | Dec 12th | | Visited 139 Ambulance at La Clytte, all hours looking well — Took over 20A Remounts at Quirepohed for D.D.R. | |
| | Dec 13th | | Saw 110 horses recently submitted by R.A. — returned at Quipphuned for Ct. Omer. Inspected 191 Coy A.S.C. & 23rd Divn. | |
| | 14th | | Took measurements of a field for supply both near Dranoutre then visited D.D.V.S. 2nd army with proposals — | |
| | 15th | | Weekly conference | |
| | 16th | | Accompanied Divisional Commander in inspection of all R.A. horses | |
| | 17th | | Visited Micmac & La Clytte transport camps — | |

# WAR DIARY
## or
## INTELLIGENCE SUMMARY
(Erase heading not required.)

Army Form C. 2118.

| Place | Date | Hour | Summary of Events and Information | Remarks and references to Appendices |
|---|---|---|---|---|
| Rumfield | 19th Dec | | Accompanied G.O.C. Division on inspection of the 123rd & 124 Inf. Brigade & the 226, 236 & 237 R.E Companies. All horses looking well. | |
| | 20th Dec | | Weekly Veterinary Conference | |
| | 26th | | Accompanied G.O.C. Division on inspection of the 122nd Infantry Bde & the Divisional Train. All well | |
| | 27th | | Examined all the horses of the 10 R.H. Units for Mange, many in very dirty state & insufficiently and & inspection on the 31st all to be washed & groomed. Inspection of break of Whitlows fever in #187 — 13 cases affected & disinfection of Divisional Wing the Money Det. | |
| | 28th | | ↑do on G.S Remounts at Rufushork ↓inspected M.V.S with Area Commandant re improvements | |

# WAR DIARY
## or
## INTELLIGENCE SUMMARY
(Erase heading not required.)

Army Form C. 2118.

| Place | Date | Hour | Summary of Events and Information | Remarks and references to Appendices |
|---|---|---|---|---|
| Renninghelst | 29th Dec | | Weekly Veterinary Conference of Divisional V.O's. | |
| | 30th Dec | | Visited D.D.V.S. 2nd Army afterwards gave a lecture to the R.A. School at Julgues on Horse management. | |
| | 31st " | | Inspected horses of 10th R.W. Kents - horses looking much better and cleaner - to be again inspected in 7 days. Inspected 228 Siege By. R.E. to settle suspicious cases of mange - arranged with Farriery to experiment further with frog caps to prevent picked up nails. | |

Goldsmith-Major
D.A.D.V.S.
II Corps.

Vol 9

War Diary
for January 1917

G. P. Knott Major A.V.C.
A.D.V.S. 41st Division

# WAR DIARY
## or
## INTELLIGENCE SUMMARY

Army Form C. 2118.

(Erase heading not required.)

| Place | Date | Hour | Summary of Events and Information | Remarks and references to Appendices |
|---|---|---|---|---|
| Remy/[?] | 1-1-17 | | Attended inspection of D.D.R. 2nd Army - Seven infantry transport horses cast as old & worn out - | |
| | | 2.45am | Owing to being unable to get a team to evacuate bad knees which were not [?] - Branch arranged with D.D.S 37 Am Ambulance (Major [?]) to [?] from [?] Own Field Amb away each day. Only two cars had the M.V.S Clear him for a day, very rarely having the O.C. [?] [?] the [?], which does not allow the [?] had staff, in proper upkeep, etc which are in a very bad state, in proper upkeep. Every bad run a again to have them [?] that might otherwise need prompt operative treatment. | |
| | | 3[?] | Visited M.V.S. - | |
| | | 4[?] | Visited Stereoid Advance Works & [?] of Am Ambulance | |

# WAR DIARY
## or
## INTELLIGENCE SUMMARY
*(Erase heading not required.)*

Army Form C. 2118.

| Place | Date | Hour | Summary of Events and Information | Remarks and references to Appendices |
|---|---|---|---|---|
| Remyfeld | 5th Jan 17 | | Visited weekly Littering Conference. | |
| | 6th Jan | | Inspecting D.A.C. horses debilitate horses to be Inoculated — all others improving — | |
| | 7th Jan | | Inspected 10th Royal Irish Rifles — Three Cases of mange to be inoculated — | |
| | 8th " | | Visited M.V.S. with Area Commandant re ordering fuel for approved. Visited 39 of R Fusiliers transport where mange had been reported. Inspected the Battalion transport offering 1/24 of 124 Solve. Disinfection & precautions to be taken — | |
| | 9th | | Receiving telephone instructions from D.D.V.S. 9 Army. That my cases that had lately become within a Rammell of firing line be inoculated — Inches M.V.S. re above — | |

Army Form C. 2118.

# WAR DIARY
## or
## INTELLIGENCE SUMMARY.
(Erase heading not required.)

| Place | Date | Hour | Summary of Events and Information | Remarks and references to Appendices |
|---|---|---|---|---|
| Rouen Pulst. | 10th Jany | | In Conjunction with the ADVS 10th Division inspected arrangements being made until Decd Stables for protection from P.O.W. huts afraid that they were satisfactory. Obtain Sulphate | |
| | 11th Jany | | proceed from to Hazebrouck. Inspect convoy of Oxteam | |
| | 12th Jany | | Weekly meeting of Divisional V.O.s | |
| | 13th Jan | | Accompanied D.A.D.O.S. to Pardoux in new Standard shed HCP + plans to carry on shoeing experiment. Plates can be fitted at less than a franc per set. In the afternoon Red General Farriers of the different formations + never mentioned | |
| | 14th Jan | | Inspected transport of 12th Brigade. Horses better still in a low state against further Grooming | |
| | 15th Jan | | Inspection from Cases of Collentis at D190 - return them to madness + free the Rem to M.V.S. | |

**Army Form C. 2118.**

# WAR DIARY
## or
## INTELLIGENCE SUMMARY.
*(Erase heading not required.)*

Instructions regarding War Diaries and Intelligence Summaries are contained in F.S. Regs., Part II. and the Staff Manual respectively. Title pages will be prepared in manuscript.

| Place | Date | Hour | Summary of Events and Information | Remarks and references to Appendices |
|---|---|---|---|---|
| Dumfries | 16th Jan 17 | | Inspected A189. Lieut O Carr & men had received part of a Remount which had joined A14 Coy on 11th inst. in transit — no inspection in all cases in transit to no inspections of engineers. | |
| | 17th Jan 17 | | Attended a Conference at Railhead. ADVS & Remounts. Inside M.V.S. in the afternoon. | |
| | 18th Jan 17 | | Arranged with Belgian Horse control Sub of horses for Hamilton purposes. Inspected M.V.S. | |
| | 19th Jan 17 | | Weekly conference of V.O.S. Visited A189 & saw all necessary steps for the control of mange after I have been taken. | |
| | 20th Jan 17 | | Attended x Coys Conference re steps to be taken if mange reappears. Suggested Immediate mange hospital treatment my Cars — difficult on the supply of clothing uniforms to men to be increased. Having attention generally. Accompanying the station veterinary officer | |

**Army Form C. 2118.**

# WAR DIARY
## or
## INTELLIGENCE SUMMARY.
*(Erase heading not required.)*

Instructions regarding War Diaries and Intelligence Summaries are contained in F. S. Regs., Part II. and the Staff Manual respectively. Title pages will be prepared in manuscript.

| Place | Date | Hour | Summary of Events and Information | Remarks and references to Appendices |
|---|---|---|---|---|
| Romy | 21st Jany | | Visited 123 Bde & 19th Midlsex although after echo employers came here have been made in the whole establishing. | |
| | 22nd Jany | | Examined all horses of the 190 Bde RFA first Hth group & Red. Am. In fact have enough even rather suspicious C.190. | |
| | 23rd Jany | | Examined 61 horses which were of the Indian army from the 4/B.M.B. Returned 16 options. 11 suspicious of mange. 3 dead. Camp. 1 welly thing. Is as not at all suspicious. Examined all the horses there by 1 Ston D.A.C. all in, any from Cavalrian Rn. from Camo & mange. | |
| | 24th Jany | | Inspected all the hospitals of the 122 Bde also his Cases of mange & the house now up there. All looking real and rich cases. | |

| | Army Form C. 2118. |
|---|---|

# WAR DIARY or INTELLIGENCE SUMMARY

(Erase heading not required.)

| Place | Date | Hour | Summary of Events and Information | Remarks and references to Appendices |
|---|---|---|---|---|
| Remingfeldt | Jan 25 - 17 | | Visited M.V.S. — | |
| | Jan 26 - 17 | | Weekly Veterinary Conference. | |
| | Jan 27 - 17 | | Inspected No 1 & No II ≡ Section S.A.C. Horses at M.L. looking well and show great improvement — No II improving very markedly still a certain number of debilitated horses — lines improving — mange ?out? & the mot Vety Section. | |
| | Jan 28 | | Inspected 226 Coys A.E. Myseing. the need slip in place are interring well & appear to be a success. | |
| | Jan 29 | | D.D.V.S. 2nd Army called & we inspected the X Corps supply bath in process — he then inspected the Construction also the 8th Corps bath complete — had them made | |
| | Jan 30 | | M.V.S. — two improvements which had been out — Ant: feeling well in dies when out. | |
| | 31 | | M.V.S. & Bickholm S.A.C. found a case of mange in Leather Mule & arranged flooring out — Inspection of all animals. | |

Vol 10

War Diaries
　　　for February 1917

G.P. Knott. Major.
　A.D.V.S. 41st Division
and O.C. 52nd Mobile Vety Section

Army Form C. 2118.

# WAR DIARY
## or
## INTELLIGENCE SUMMARY.
(Erase heading not required.)

| Place | Date | Hour | Summary of Events and Information | Remarks and references to Appendices |
|---|---|---|---|---|
| Rumfeldt | Feb 1-17 | | Inspected all animals of B. Echelon D.A.C. having horses a cage of mange on the day previously, rapid cases of mange amongst B. horses on the day previously. Arranged for 2 section clipping being issued. Require clipping horses in companies horses. | |
| | Feb 2nd | | Inspected W.I & II. Sections D.A.C. & 124th Bde Transport lines — | |
| | Feb 3rd | | Inspected sick lines of 189th Bde R.F.A. — | |
| | Feb 4th | | Transport horses of 123 Bde Mange to three swim of Inspected cases of mange to be sent to the M.V.S. also a reply to M.O.E. told Tolg. — | |
| | Feb 5th | | Inspected 187 Bde R.F.A. All Batterie much improved except B. which still has a number of thin horses — Found a fresh case of mange in A — but returned of Suspicion of mange. | |

Army Form C. 2118.

# WAR DIARY
## or
## INTELLIGENCE SUMMARY.
(Erase heading not required.)

Instructions regarding War Diaries and Intelligence Summaries are contained in F. S. Regs., Part II. and the Staff Manual respectively. Title pages will be prepared in manuscript.

| Place | Date | Hour | Summary of Events and Information | Remarks and references to Appendices |
|---|---|---|---|---|
| Dunkirk | Feb 1st | | Visited B. Echelon D.A.C. Clothing held up owing to faulty tags. Arranged with D.A.D.O.S. to have all the heads sent to Calais until further necessary in order to save time. Mules suffer without ice. 10%. | |
| " | 4th | | Inspected 189th Bde F.B.A.C. | |
| | | | D 189 - Horses only fair - 3 suspects | |
| | | | C 189 - Horses excellent condition - 2 suspects | |
| | | | B 189 - Horses fair - 3 suspects | |
| | | | A 189 - Horses good - one debility - 2 suspects | |
| | | | B.A.C. - Animals good - 1 mange - 3 suspects | |
| | 8th | | Inspected No 1 Section D.A.C. Horses in good condition. Visited Poperinghe Horse dips in afternoon. | |
| | 9th | | Took over 97 Remounts from D.R. in morning. In afternoon attended weekly Vety Conference. | |

# WAR DIARY
## INTELLIGENCE SUMMARY

Army Form C. 2118.

| Place | Date | Hour | Summary of Events and Information | Remarks and references to Appendices |
|---|---|---|---|---|
| Rennefeld | 10th Feb 17 | | Visited M.V.S. transport lines shed had been heated for mange for the discharges - one horse which had been admitted for Debility during a.m. P.m. was found to have had injected with Strongylus armatus. This may be a rare chance of Death. Item no reports - | |
| | 11th Feb 17 | | Inspected 1.2.3 Bde transport = 10th R.W.R. cub. & 2b Artillerage horses not highly arranged to Crushed oats 40 horses & 20 horses respectively. Two no clothing with Hd Qrs Debility. One of these horses was at least twenty five years old - | |
| | 12th | | Attended M.V.S. P.C. being in bed with Cold. | |
| | 13th | | Inspected Regnal & Head Qb lines, looking well. | |
| | 14th | | Visited duffen Bath at P.Mepanghi, in order to make arrangements | |
| | | | Thanks of this Summer - | |
| | 15th | | Attended horse demonstration at It Omen. | |

**Army Form C. 2118.**

# WAR DIARY
## or
## INTELLIGENCE SUMMARY
*(Erase heading not required.)*

| Place | Date | Hour | Summary of Events and Information | Remarks and references to Appendices |
|---|---|---|---|---|
| Romford | 10 Feb 17 | | Inspection B & A.C. & A.C. Horseshoes then clipping - | |
| | 17th | | Inspection 190 Bde R.F.A - | |
| | | | A Battery, Post-evolution, 2 Schiths, 3 hours - Illuminated the during A. | |
| | | | B " fair " 2 " 5 " | |
| | | | C " Good " 1 " 6 " | |
| | | | D " fair " 2 " 1 " | |
| | | | The Bde has been in wet camp for a week. Horses one M. Standing in the open during very cold weather. Have applied for Canada rets - | 50 for A. 20 for B. 20 for C. 40 - D. |

Army Form C. 2118.

# WAR DIARY
## or
## INTELLIGENCE SUMMARY.
(Erase heading not required.)

| Place | Date | Hour | Summary of Events and Information | Remarks and references to Appendices |
|---|---|---|---|---|
| Remyfield | 18th Feb 17. | | Inspected Ramparts, 1,2,3 Bn. Infantry — Decidedly Quiet — the 10th R.W.K. as a whole which was Appleton with Brange was to find cases continually coming up. | |
| | 19th " | | Stood up 15 horses to D.D.R mostly old age & Vice, they were cast — Attended the Supper hat/9th VIII Corps when the Allen Munds Did in Dinner was offered — R.A. R.E. D.T. & Infantry think the O.C. M.V.S Sgt. Kicked in the neck by a horse — removed to the Field Ambulance — | |
| | 20th " | | Three Suppers hat/ VIII Corps attending the M.V.S — Took over Remts at Hurpronts from 2.D.17 — | |
| | 21st " | | Opened a Dummy Mange Stable | |
| | 22nd " | | Inspected horses going through dipping bath at Pfluenyhe — Took over Remts from 2.B.R. | |

# WAR DIARY
## or
## INTELLIGENCE SUMMARY

Army Form C. 2118.

| Place | Date | Hour | Summary of Events and Information | Remarks and references to Appendices |
|---|---|---|---|---|
| Ronveflet | 23 Feb 17 | | Inspected 18/1320 R.F.A. at Reyveld — when the Bdye were supposed to be "in rest" — Five horses had been drowned in the No 2 nature the distressed as bolanted — Pynter water to S.O.C. the parade it to Cypo — Horse Lectures | |
| | 24th | | B1 gun Cyple & a dinner him dressed — H Amm Supply — Horse which had been sent for them begin with Reparing — | |
| | 25th | | Inform cases shown me So put - were with Reparing — Horse Stable — 9 inspected head Q's horse — | |
| | 26th | | Inspected 123 Iny. Bde. with Genl Inglis — arranged renewal | |
| | 27th | | H Arni. A'd Amm, horses of Bde improving — | |
| | 28th | | Horse Lecture — Erected a Spraying apparatus | |

Aphtuth Major

# WAR DIARY
## INTELLIGENCE SUMMARY

ADVS 41 Div Vol XI

| Place | Date | Hour | Summary of Events and Information | Remarks and references to Appendices |
|---|---|---|---|---|
| Reninghelst | March 1/17 | | Continued dealing with correspondence of V.O.s. | |
| | 2nd | | Weekly conference of V.O.s. | |
| | 3rd | | Still dealing with work in room. | |
| | 4th | | Handed over office to Lt. I.C. M.V.S. | |
| | 5th | | Lindup leave. | |
| | 6th | | Proceeded to Huts for Inspection of Inspection by the D.D.R. Veterinary Army & the Inspecting Surgeons | |
| | 9th | 10" | of the 123rd Brigade at the 52nd M.V.Sub Sections BELL Pt POPERINGHE. | |
| | 10" | 2:34 | Horses were inspected at the VIII Corps BATT POPERINGHE | |
| | 12" | | Inspection of the Artillery of the 41st Division by the D.V.S | |
| | | | occupied by the D.D.V.S Second Army | |
| | 16" | | Weekly conference of V.O.s | |
| | 17" | | Certain of 187 Brigade R.F.A by D.D.V.S Second Army | |
| | 18" | | Vlabery Inspection of 12 mules R.H at ST JAN-CAPPEL | |

**Army Form C. 2118.**

# WAR DIARY
## or
## INTELLIGENCE SUMMARY.
*(Erase heading not required.)*

| Place | Date | Hour | Summary of Events and Information | Remarks and references to Appendices |
|---|---|---|---|---|
| Remyfelst | March 19th | | Returned from leave. | |
| | 20th | | Attended Conference of D.D.V.S. 2d Army at Bailleul, subject of abnormal death of horses & ships. See Item 16. | |
| | 21st | | Inspected 1st & 2nd Divl. R.F.A. — A large number of debilitated owing to exposure during "stay in" Ridd. Area — No shelter. Standing up. | |
| | 22nd | | Inspected in AEC — all water & sopp depôts. Both in process of erection. | |
| | 23rd | | Inspected No 2 Section D.A.C. — Weekly conference of V.O.s. | |
| | 24th | | Attended casting board H.Q. D.D.R. — In every inspection at D.H.Q. | |
| | 25th | | Attended inspection by G.O.C. of 190 Bde R.F.A. & 123 Bde Infantry. Both have far too many Italian horses — None arranged for. | |
| | | | Want of houses Sidi & Arable rats — G.O.C. transport in a months time. | |
| | 26th | | Visited VIII Corps supply baths & ADVS & DY Division. | |
| | 27th | | Inspected B. Echelon D.A.C. — Arrange for forced evacuation — | |
| | 28 | | " No 1 Section D.A.C. dto " " | |

# WAR DIARY
## or
## INTELLIGENCE SUMMARY.

*(Erase heading not required.)*

Army Form C. 2118.

| Place | Date | Hour | Summary of Events and Information | Remarks and references to Appendices |
|---|---|---|---|---|
| Rawal Pindi | March 29 | | Camp and horses D.2.& Coy R.E. & W. Coy A.S.C. which had remained with Plain Dist Scales. Inspn at all satisfactory. Reported tho matter to A.O.V.S. | |
| | 30 | | Visited 9th Coy Supply batt. efficients & Coys Q. Services remanded for Coys Battle. Also A.O.V.S. Coys. | |
| | 31st | | Chiefly compsn of Coy Battle V.O.L. Inspected 123 Pack Transport. Annuals commencing to improve though still in stable management | |

Ebhult Major
A.D.V.S. 2i Division

War Diaries
 for April 1917

G.P. Knott. Major

 A.D.V.S. 41st Division

O.C. 52nd Mobile Veterinary Section

Vol 12

# WAR DIARY
## of
## INTELLIGENCE SUMMARY.
(Erase heading not required.)

Army Form C. 2118.

| Place | Date | Hour | Summary of Events and Information | Remarks and references to Appendices |
|---|---|---|---|---|
| Rumilly | April 1st | | Inspected transport B 123 Bde Infantry - much improved - | |
| | 2nd | | Inspected M.V.S - Divisional Scabies Stable - | |
| | 3 | | Inspected Hd: Section D.A.C. - 10th Corps Dipping Bath - Divisional Scabies Stable. Met with an accident, horse | |
| | 4. | | slipped up & falling on my leg - | |
| | 5 | | Visited + Corps Dipping Bath with the D.D.V.S. | |
| | 6 | | Weekly Conference of V.O.S - | |
| | 7. | | Inspected B Battery 189 A.F.A. Recommended 75-horses being put on extra rations - many debilitated owing to exposure - | |
| | 8. | | Inspected of 124 Infantry Brigade by O.C. Dunn - Animals in excellent condition. Divisional Scabies Stable - | |
| | 9. | | M.V.S. Divisional Scabies Stable - | |
| | 10. | | Inspected No 192. D.A.C. animals in good condition - | |

**Army Form C. 2118.**

# WAR DIARY
## or
## INTELLIGENCE SUMMARY
*(Erase heading not required.)*

Instructions regarding War Diaries and Intelligence Summaries are contained in F.S. Regs., Part II. and the Staff Manual respectively. Title pages will be prepared in manuscript.

| Place | Date | Hour | Summary of Events and Information | Remarks and references to Appendices |
|---|---|---|---|---|
| Reninghelst | April 12th | | Inspected A & D Batteries 187 Bde R.F.A. — Horses fast improving — riding horse done to improve condition of debilitated horse. — Debilitated horse placed in separate stable given | |
| | | | B horse feed. — Debilitated horse reports weekly to G.O.C. Division who is dealing with the matter. | |
| | | | Care being taken. Reporter weekly to G.O.C. Division who is dealing with the matter. | |
| | 13th | | M.V.S. & Debility Stable. Horses improving — | |
| | 14th | | Inspected C & B Batteries 187 Bde R.F.A. — | |
| | 15th | | Inspected with the G.O.C. Division the 187th Bde R.F.A. & the 228, 233 & 237 Companies of the R.E. Regiment. | |
| | | | Debilitated horses now being formed on farm here | |
| | 16 | | Inspected five horses of Belgian artillery rough all fit alongside owing to old age & extreme debility. — | |

# WAR DIARY
## or
## INTELLIGENCE SUMMARY
*(Erase heading not required.)*

Army Form C. 2118.

| Place | Date | Hour | Summary of Events and Information | Remarks and references to Appendices |
|---|---|---|---|---|
| Renighelst | April 17th | | Inspected D Battery of the 189 Bde AFA which had been in having area. Marching in the open without respect to standing orders. Ordered destruction of three horse chestnut whistles & arrangements for cleaned lots for [?] men. Lines in bad condition — Six cases of colic had just occurred. P.M. stood against inflammation of mucus & large intestines — mainly due to mouldy hay which had been given as chaff. Handed over to Capt Liles. Proceeded to left new mob of DOVS. 2 Army who is going on leave | |
| | | 20ᵗʰ | 135 horses were sent to no 3 horse Dip at SANS CAPPEL | |
| | | 3H | 20 horses were sent to the horse Dip at POPERINGHE | |

… Army Form C. 2118.

# WAR DIARY
## or
## INTELLIGENCE SUMMARY.
*(Erase heading not required.)*

| Place | Date | Hour | Summary of Events and Information | Remarks and references to Appendices |
|---|---|---|---|---|
| BENINGHELST | April 27 | 19.5 | Horses were sent to dispose D/o at JAN'S CAPPEL | |

M.B. Dalyson A.V.C.
For Major Rathe
A.D.V.S.

Vol 13

War Diaries
for May 1917

G.P. Knott - Major. A.D.V.S. 41st Division
~~O.C. 52nd M.V.S.~~

# WAR DIARY
## or
## INTELLIGENCE SUMMARY
*(Erase heading not required.)*

Army Form C. 2118.

| Place | Date | Hour | Summary of Events and Information | Remarks and references to Appendices |
|---|---|---|---|---|
| Renninghelst | 3/5/17 | | Returning from doing duty for the D.D.V.S. 2nd Army who was absent on leave – Visited Belgian Artillery who a number of horses were reported to be suffering from poison, suspicion that been produced by anuag eating horse cake – Two had died many up in appearance of acute gastritis, sickness, stiffness of then head, temp of horses went fifty, intestines taken off by Capts Mathias for analysis. Morant & Intestines taken off by Capts Mathias for analysis. | |
| | 4/5/17 | | Horses are without fifty of them had been under by D.D.V.S. who took acute symptoms – They had under by D.D.V.S. who took Mr Semples over for analysis – Inspected 190 Bell R.F.A. | |
| | 5/5/17 | | Belgian Artillery horses improving – no new acute case – they are treated with – Pilocarpine & Pil Hyd & Tod 46 M.V.S. – notified by General O.i.C. also complaints to be evaluated of suffering | |

# WAR DIARY or INTELLIGENCE SUMMARY

Army Form C. 2118.

| Place | Date | Hour | Summary of Events and Information | Remarks and references to Appendices |
|---|---|---|---|---|
| Ruyaulcourt | 6-8-17. | | Visited Debility Section of M.V.S. All horses improving — | |
| | 7-8-17. | | Attended a Demonstration at Dernancourt Gas School of shewing the methods of attaching the new Respirators for horses — | |
| | 8-5-17. | | Inspected Sore horses of A/187. have had been killed with Shell wounds and fifteen wounded — the gunner of Battery has now been changed — Inspected the 228 - 233 - 237 Bys; R.E., the 228 & the 237 are both looking well, the 233 Bys horses are not improving, after the weather the H.A.A. M.G. I recommend the Bmy O.C. being changed, he is in fact as a Stable Manager | |

# WAR DIARY
## or
## INTELLIGENCE SUMMARY.
(Erase heading not required.)

Army Form C. 2118.

| Place | Date | Hour | Summary of Events and Information | Remarks and references to Appendices |
|---|---|---|---|---|
| Renneghelst | 9-5-17 | | Inspected the 122 Inf. Bde at Reninghelst area. All animals about well - also C 187 Bde RFA. Attended fire to D Form Rennes- known to him to have - three inspected and also B Bucks - Inspected W 1 & 2 Sections D.A.C. Both looking well. | |
| | 10-5-17 | | Went particularly to D - still leading but have Visited Dipping bath hut (X Coy) still leading and have occasional instructions to give it a trial with 5 pigs - will not be surprised if it tell in & kills no of men - in afternoon would weekly veterinary conference - It seems upon that the D Battery horses of 187 Bde are losing condition owing insufficient men looking after them. I reported units to AA & QMG- who sent up flying | |
| | 11-5-17 | | Col. Taylor at Poperinghe — all men on lectures in the lines — | |

Army Form C. 2118.

# WAR DIARY
## or
## INTELLIGENCE SUMMARY.
(Erase heading not required.)

| Place | Date | Hour | Summary of Events and Information | Remarks and references to Appendices |
|---|---|---|---|---|
| Rumpfus | 12-5-17 | | Inspected Belgian Artillery with D.A.D.R. Inspected B & O Batteries 187 Bde, whose Batteries the horses are looking in condition owing to inexperienced men to look after them, large numbers of men being employed in the front line, sent a written report on subject to Head Qtrs — | |
| | 13-5-17 | | Visited the X Corps Depôt, horses hutched & Dilluth Stable — | |
| | 15-5-17 | | Supped so horses to H.A. X Corps on X Corps Rest. The both leaving 9 in during two hours of work. 19 by next morning — | |
| | 16-5-17 | | Inspected No 2 Section J.A.C. & the 124th Hy. Bde. All animals looking well & in good condition — | |
| | 17-5-17 | | Visited M.V.S. & Dilluth Stable | |
| | 18-5-17 | | Weekly Veterinary Conference | |
| | 19-5-17 | | Inspected 190 Bde R.F.A., also 123 Fd Bde, all much improved except the D/H. OAbe 123 Bde — | |

**Army Form C. 2118.**

# WAR DIARY
## or
## INTELLIGENCE SUMMARY
*(Erase heading not required.)*

Instructions regarding War Diaries and Intelligence Summaries are contained in F.S. Regs., Part II. and the Staff Manual respectively. Title pages will be prepared in manuscript.

| Place | Date | Hour | Summary of Events and Information | Remarks and references to Appendices |
|---|---|---|---|---|
| Review/det | 20-5-19 | | Visited the Divisional Artillery Staff — Examined 137 A.D. Remounts for R.A. a fair lot. | |
| | 21/5/19 | | Inspected with O.O.C. 123 Bde Inf. Remounts. Arrived a demonstration of Horse falling. Velocite hands of some Cases. Pouring Rain for inspn. a.u.c. Pelock needs inducing anything. From the two Plants. Also Remounts induced anything. Inspected by 103 Bng. D.T. Horses. In both Cases horses become eaten — many black work. Reported the matter in writing to H.Q. | |
| | 22-5-19 | | Visited O X Corps with Dep. of Studying out all the Defence Plans at the X Corps Horse Bath and Glue's cleaned. all Horses the returned & Mules. Anglech Plant down. About a hundred & five horses having been suffy — Inspected 136 Ambulance. Annuals all fit for work. Ambulation plan. | |
| | 23-5-17 | | Inspected Div. Annuals of 124 Bde Inf. in Shelp- Area. | |
| | 24-5-17 | | Inspected 122 Inf. Bn. All annuals in very good condition — | |
| | 25-5-17 | | Visited S.O.S. Divnrl. R.A. 12 AFA & 6 SAFA. all of which will now be Permanent they met — | |
| | 26/5/17 | | Visited S.O. & O. FA.— Reported to Branch to assist making arrangements Attended Divisional Conference. | |

# WAR DIARY
## or
## INTELLIGENCE SUMMARY
(Erase heading not required.)

Army Form C. 2118.

| Place | Date | Hour | Summary of Events and Information | Remarks and references to Appendices |
|---|---|---|---|---|
| Ennefibel | 27/5/17 | | Visited D D O & I Army - re evacuations during offensive. | |
| | 28/5/17 | | Inspected 1st Divisional R.A. — 2nd Bde. RFA — 113 Battery Horses in good condition and well cared for as the evacuate for debility. 114th Battery Condition Improving, horses improved - 1 for debility, 1 for rifle wound - 2 evacuations for debility, 2 evacuations for death. 115th Battery Horses apply to this Battery - 2 for the Veterinary Section — 1 for evacuation for mange, 1 for debility. 2nd Battery — Ditto — 1 for evacuation for mange, 1 for debility. 39th Bde. R.F.A. All the horses of this Brigade are looking well & are well cared for. It being only necessary to evacuate one for debility. | |

# WAR DIARY
## or
## INTELLIGENCE SUMMARY

| Place | Date | Hour | Summary of Events and Information | Remarks and references to Appendices |
|---|---|---|---|---|
| Runnyfeld | 29/5/17 | | Inspected the 126th A.F.A. Bde. — Holding in Debility — Inoculated 15 of the unit forming Reinfs anneh the divinl — Reported in writing to D.D.V.S. 2nd Army. | |
| | 30/5/17 | | Inspected the 6D - A.F.A. Bde. the B.A.C. 9 B122 B139 Batty horses made way in the whole in good condition — the A.S 29 B.S.D Batter horses in finer condition - Special horses particularly in DSD have long than hulet - was only necessary to inoculate five — | |
| | 31/5/17 | | Inspected the 42 Bett # F.A — Condition the horses fair but there were several horses suffering with debility that picked had been evacuated All and their horse case of mange - arranged for the immediate evacuation of 35 Cases — Visited by DDVS or Veteriny arrangements for inoculated during offensive — | |

R.P. Hunt Major AOVS 21 Div

# WAR DIARY
## INTELLIGENCE SUMMARY

D ARV S 4/

| Place | Date | Hour | Summary of Events and Information | Remarks |
|---|---|---|---|---|
| Remiencourt | 1/6/17 | | India M.V.S. – Usual weekly Conference of V.O.s | |
| | 2/6/17 | | Divisional Horse Show – M.V.S. Exhibits given 1st & 2nd prize – | |
| | 3/6/17 | | Inspected the 277 Bde A.F.A. – Animals in good condition except Canadians – Only one horse for evacuation – | |
| | 4/6/17 | | Inspected B. Echelon S.A.C. 41 Div. – All animals in very good condition. Only one animal for mud & mange. Still mounted. 41st Divisional trains, inspected the four Companies, general improvement – | |
| | 5-6-17 | | Since last inspection, owing to decrease in work – Visited 2 Canadian Laundry Company & see two horses reported to be suffering with shrapnel wounds. Evacuated them to M.V.S. – Inspected the 228. 233 & 237 Coys R.E. all much improved since last inspection especially the 233 Coy – | |
| | 6-6-17 | | Inspected D.M.V.S. – | |
| | 7/6/17 | | Inspection B 228 & 237 Coys R.E. Lose deaths from shrapnel & 22 hundred horses taken place during the night – | |

# WAR DIARY
## INTELLIGENCE SUMMARY
*(Erase heading not required.)*

Army Form C. 2118.

| Place | Date | Hour | Summary of Events and Information | Remarks and references to Appendices |
|---|---|---|---|---|
| Rebruyhlist | 8/6/17 | | 2nd Lieut. Weekly Veterinary Conference — | |
| | 9/6/17 | | India M.V.S. | |
| | 10/6/17 | | Inspection B. Battery 190 Bde. when instead, change of interior pasture. Rest Cattle Returned from Army Schools. Found 34 slightly affected cases. Infection further got out. 11 further severe cases being evacuated. 11 Suspicious Cases — The few more severe cases (for treatment). Arrangements made for treatment of remainder. | |
| | 11/6/17 | | Inspection 111 Behn. S.A.C. all animals in good condition except a number with Cellulitis — Evacuation for m. units. putting in with the large horse. Visits to 190 Bde him they were. All cases of M.V.S. & abt. 10 — | |
| | 12/6/17 | | Made arrangements for evacuation of sick cases of M.V.S. on trains. The inning of the M.V.S. on trains. | |
| | 13/6/17 | | Visits 5. 2. A. F. A. Bde. Horses improving. Three Lyth. Cases Pneumonia. Arranged for removal of the M.V.S. to N.Y.A.S. — | |

# WAR DIARY
## INTELLIGENCE SUMMARY
*(Erase heading not required.)*

Army Form C. 2118.

| Place | Date | Hour | Summary of Events and Information | Remarks and references to Appendices |
|---|---|---|---|---|
| Rahmyfeld | 14/6/17 | | J. J. Reed. Inspected the Animals of the 26 A.F.A. Bde. The condition of the animals & General management have much improved since my last inspection report - Date 28th May 17 | |
| | 15/6/17 | | Inspection of 72 & 73 Bde A.F.A. gave instructions for the immediate Q. Fhms suffering from debility including two horses gone of Ryedia to G.S.13. Ration this bde should put a stop to all horses in a bad condition. | |
| | 16/6/17 | | Was rung up by Q.I.O. R.A. & info. stating he did not agree with increasing to various horses of the 72nd Bde vmas leaving the Corps Area before Genl Brewis handed me to meet him - Regretted the matter the army, who concurred the decision of the Corps put - I then had a report that the whole matter for a ruling by the Army Commandt. | |

# WAR DIARY or INTELLIGENCE SUMMARY

Army Form C. 2118.

| Place | Date | Hour | Summary of Events and Information | Remarks and references to Appendices |
|---|---|---|---|---|
| Remy Judet | 17/6/17 | | to Sheet | |
| | | | India M.V.S. convoyed movement to IV Corps C.C.S. arrived a.o.s. ? x app — | |
| | 18/6/17 | | Reported to x app — Arrange State of appointment in the 2nd. | |
| | | | Reached our place. Went to O.C. M.V.S. who took O.C. A.D.M.S. | |
| | 19.6.17 | | Ditto | |
| | 20.6.17 | | Capt. C.W.B. Sikes took over from a.d. Knott to act. O.C. D.A.D.Y.S. | |
| | 22.6.17 | | B.D. Bellevue 1.9 Brigade and about 186 P. Bury are 6.D Bellevue 1.9 Brigade div at ST. JANS CAPPEL. A.F.A. were but through Veterinary Officers. Inspection of Veterinary Officers a groupsam of 128 ry auxty Brigade | |
| | 23.6.17 | | D.A.D.V.S. moved from REMINGHELST to WESTOUTRE 1st Field Ambulance | |
| | 26.6.17 | | 10m horses 1 190th Brigade & 10 mules 124 infantry Bug are were examined. 4r. ST. JANS. CAPPEL. | |

Army Form C. 2118.

# WAR DIARY
## or
## INTELLIGENCE SUMMARY.
(Erase heading not required.)

| Place | Date | Hour | Summary of Events and Information | Remarks and references to Appendices |
|---|---|---|---|---|
| | 28.6.19 | | 3rd D.A.D.V.S. | |
| | 29.6.19 | | Visited M.V.S. to arrange evacuation | |
| | | | Conference of Veterinary Officers | |
| | 30.6.19 | | Came to Britain to see casting to M.V.S. | |
| | | | Attended conference at Standard Store Quarters | |

W.B. DeNos
Capt.
3/D.A.D.V.S.

War Diary
for July 1917

C.W.B. Sikes. Major. M.B.
A.D.L.V.S. 41st Division.

# WAR DIARY
## or
## INTELLIGENCE SUMMARY.
(Erase heading not required.)

Army Form C. 2118.

| Place | Date | Hour | Summary of Events and Information | Remarks and references to Appendices |
|---|---|---|---|---|
| WESTOUTRE | 1.9.17 | | G Sec. moved to BERTHEN. | |
| BERTHEN | 2.9.17 | | Visited 253 Coy R.E. | |
| | 3.9.17 | | Visited 257 and 258 Coys R.E. and 20 Burmese Coy Infy. | |
| | 4.9.17 | | Inspected 132 Coy Infy Brigade & Special Coys at X.19.1.1. where Stores had been in readiness of formation's at VLAMERTINGHE. | |
| | 6.9.17 | | Visited D.D. Works X Corps | |
| | 7.9.17 | | Attended a conference at VLAMERTINGHE visited 19 & Mullhouse Pioneer | |
| | 8.9.17 | | Inspected to H.Q. D.A.C. Cavalry | |
| | 9.9.17 | | Visited H.Q. Green Traffic Control & Cavalry H.Q. 87 Brigade | |
| | 10.9.17 | | O Sychicy & Approach Routes at St JANS CAPPEL. | |

Army Form C. 2118.

# WAR DIARY
## or
## INTELLIGENCE SUMMARY.
*(Erase heading not required.)*

Instructions regarding War Diaries and Intelligence Summaries are contained in F.S. Regs., Part II. and the Staff Manual respectively. Title pages will be prepared in manuscript.

| Place | Date | Hour | Summary of Events and Information | Remarks and references to Appendices |
|---|---|---|---|---|
| BERTHEN | 11.7.14 | | 21st July | |
| | 13.7.14 | | Inspected 190 F. Brigade Bay ale | |
| | 14.7.14 | | Inspected 134 Infantry Bay ale | |
| | 15.7.14 | | Inspected 133 Infantry Bay ale | |
| | 16.7.14 | | Inspected H.1st Divisional Train | |
| | 17.7.14 | | Inspected 156 Remounts | |
| | | | Losses etc. of JANS KAPPEL | |
| | 19.7.14 | | Conference of Veterinary Officers | |
| | | | Attendance M.V.S. to George & evacuation. | |
| | 21.7.14 | | Palembe 238 Machine gun Company | |
| | 23.7.14 | | Mobile Vety Section Arrive to CA, LATTE N° A 85 | |
| | 25.7.14 | | Officers horses to ourey WESTOUTRE | |
| WESTOUTRE | 26.7.14 | | Inference H Veterinary Officers | |
| | | | attended M.P.S to ourey Deracuation | |
| | 27.7.14 | | Visit VOORMEZEELE to attend wounded horses. | |

**Army Form C. 2118.**

# WAR DIARY
## or
## INTELLIGENCE SUMMARY.
(Erase heading not required.)

Instructions regarding War Diaries and Intelligence Summaries are contained in F. S. Regs., Part II. and the Staff Manual respectively. Title pages will be prepared in manuscript.

| Place | Date | Hour | Summary of Events and Information | Remarks and references to Appendices |
|---|---|---|---|---|
| WESTOUTRE | 28.7.17 | | 3rd Cdn. Sept. 29 Reinforcements attended M.V.S. to arrange evacuation by rail. | |
| | 29.7.17 | | Visited 139 Field Ambulance at VIERSTRAAT Visited M.V.S. to arrange evacuation | |
| | 30.7.17 | | Inspected 128 Infantry Brigade | |
| | 31.7.17 | | Visited VOERMEZEELE to select an advanced dressing station. | |

W[?] Dittos
Maj. DADVS.

Vol 16

War Diaries
for August 1917

C.W.B. Sikes. Major A.V.C.
D.A.D.V.S. 41st Division.
O.C. 52nd M.V.S.

Army Form C. 2118.

# WAR DIARY
## or
## INTELLIGENCE SUMMARY.

(Erase heading not required.)

| Place | Date | Hour | Summary of Events and Information | Remarks and references to Appendices |
|---|---|---|---|---|
| WESTOUTRE | 1.8.17 | | Visited D.A.D.V.S. 4th Divison to arrange for Personnel for advanced dressing post. | |
| | 2.8.17 | | Reconnoitred dressing post. Was established at H 30 d 1.3 Visited Mobile Veterinary Section for evacuating sick D.R. horses to Army to dispose of. Supplying Gases CR4PDR 125 oz of Sulky Brigade Y 2.38 Machine Gun Company | |
| | 3.8.17 | | Visited M.V.S. Attended conference at D.H.Q. | |
| | 4.8.17 | | Visited YPRES to inspect Ambulance when in use. Inspected advanced dressing station. | |
| | 5.8.17 | | Visited WIPPENHOEK to entrain prisoners for the base. | |
| | 6.8.17 | | Visited M.V.S. | |
| | 7.8.17 | | Inspected 187 Brigade | |
| | 8.8.17 | | Inspection of M.K.S. by Gen Moore accompanied by Capt Wilson and lst Lt H. Knott. | |

# WAR DIARY
## or
## INTELLIGENCE SUMMARY
(Erase heading not required.)

Army Form C. 2118.

| Place | Date | Hour | Summary of Events and Information | Remarks and references to Appendices |
|---|---|---|---|---|
| WESTOUTRE | 8.8.17 | | Going to the advanced dressing Stny badly shelled. J-was. at the Ky. H. 30 d. 13 in Shelter H 30 c.3.8. | |
| | 9.8.17 | | Absence of Veterinary Officers | |
| | 10.8.17 | | Opp Surg 190 Bde arr'd and reported. Rode up to inspect Dr of wing between lines of a Cas ? trenches by B Buxry Ferm. & close vicinity. Several cases of influenza diseases reg'd. | |
| | 11.8.17 | | Visited 138 Fd Ambulance and M.V.S. | |
| | 12.8.17 | | Visited Mobile Vety Section | |
| | 13.8.17 | | Visited 133 rgt J. JANS CAPPEL | |
| | 14.8.17 | | D/Supp'y Anned BERTHEN. | |
| | 15.8.17 | | Officer 138 Fd Ambulance J.D.A.C. | |
| | 16.8.17 | | Inspection of 48 Renumts | |

Army Form C. 2118.

# WAR DIARY
## or
## INTELLIGENCE SUMMARY.
(Erase heading not required.)

Instructions regarding War Diaries and Intelligence Summaries are contained in F. S. Regs. Part II. and the Staff Manual respectively. Title pages will be prepared in manuscript.

| Place | Date | Hour | Summary of Events and Information | Remarks and references to Appendices |
|---|---|---|---|---|
| BERTHEN | 18.8.17 | | Major C.W.B. SIKES, D.A.D.V.S. left on 10 days leave to ENGLAND. Captain J.F. MACDONALD A.V.C. O.C. 52nd M.V.S. took over as acting D.A.D.V.S. during Major SIKES absence, & visited the 124 Infantry Brigade, 234 R.F.B., No. 2 Coy. M.D.V. Train, & 140 Field Ambulance. | |
| | 19.8.17 | | Visited 122nd Infantry Brigade & 238 Machine Gun Co., & Divisional H.Q. Signal Coy. | |
| | 20.8.17. | | 52nd M.V.S. marched from BERTHEN to camp south of HONDEGHEM. | |
| | 21.8.17. | | 52nd M.V.S. marched from HONDEGHEM to WIZERNES & took over from 1/2 LONDON M.V.S. Office moved from BERTHEN to WIZERNES. | |
| WIZERNES | 22.8.17. | | Visited 122 Infantry Brigade & 52nd M.V.S. | |
| | 23.8.17. | | Visited 52nd M.V.S. Conference of V.Os. at office. | |
| | 24.8.17. | | Visited 52nd M.V.S. & H.Q. Signal Coy. | |

# WAR DIARY
## or
## INTELLIGENCE SUMMARY.

Army Form C. 2118.

| Place | Date | Hour | Summary of Events and Information | Remarks and references to Appendices |
|---|---|---|---|---|
| WIZERNES | 25.8.17 | | Visited 122 Infantry Brigade & 52nd M.V.S. | |
| | 26.8.17 | | Visited No. 2 Coy. 41 Div. Train & 52nd M.V.S. | |
| | 27.8.17 | | Evacuated 10 animals to No. 23 Veterinary Hospital. Visited 52nd M.V.S. & H.Q. Signal Coy. | |
| | 28.8.17 | | Visited 124 Infantry Brigade & 52nd M.V.S. | |
| | 29.8.17 | | Major C. W. B. Giffes A.V.C. returned from 10 days leave | |
| | 30.8.17 | | Inspected Veterinary Officers of Infantry Brigade. | |
| | 31.8.17 | | Inspected P.33 O.R. of Army Troops a.s. | |

M.B. Giffes
Major DADVS

War Diary for Sept 1917
C.W.B. Sikes, Major A.V.C.
D.A.D.V.S. 41st Division
and O.C. 52nd Mobile Veterinary Section

**Army Form C. 2118.**

# WAR DIARY
## or
## INTELLIGENCE SUMMARY.
*(Erase heading not required.)*

Instructions regarding War Diaries and Intelligence Summaries are contained in F. S. Regs., Part II. and the Staff Manual respectively. Title pages will be prepared in manuscript.

| Place | Date | Hour | Summary of Events and Information | Remarks and references to Appendices |
|---|---|---|---|---|
| WIZERNES | 1.9.17 | | O.C. & Adjt. Inspected 123 & O'Clucrty Brigades and 190 Inf Brigade Trans. D.D. & Mon. | |
| | 3.9.17 | | O.C. Inspected 134 & Mon. Inf Brigade and No 4 Coy A.S.C. | |
| | 4.9.17 | | Visited all field ambulances & 55 Veterinary Hospital | |
| | 5.9.17 | | Examined No. 23 Infantry Brigade at D.H.Q. | |
| | 6.9.17 | | Attended O.J. (123 D.) O.C. & Adjt Brigade | |
| | 7.9.17 | | Inspected 138 Equitation Court Pty. | |
| | 8.9.17 | | Visited 30 Divl Amm Sqn. & 131 Brigade and 138 Coy L.T.R 123 O.C. & Adjt Bomby Repair | |
| | 9.9.17 | | | |
| | 10.9.17 | | 1400 Indian Ambulance Coy Bomby Repair Inspected 53 Remounts HMM 128 whom here one of whom complaining Visited 11 R.N.F. Ind. Rf. Camp 133 Machine Gun Coy | |
| | 11.9.17 | | Attended Mobile Vety Sect. | |
| | 13.9.17 | | Visited LA CLYTTE & West Preston in Mobile | |
| | 15.9.17 | | Vety Gun Awy | |

# WAR DIARY
## or
## INTELLIGENCE SUMMARY.

*(Erase heading not required.)*

Army Form C. 2118.

| Place | Date | Hour | Summary of Events and Information | Remarks and references to Appendices |
|---|---|---|---|---|
| WIZERNES | 13.9.17 | | L. Shell. Inspected Veterinary Officers | |
| | 14.9.17 | | Mobile Veterinary Section though went 135 to Sanday Brigade. Rode to LA FAYETTE. | |
| | 15.9.17 | | Rode around B & C/69th D.A.C. Inspected H.B. & C/69 Bgde and I am & Lahore Section of 190 Bgde. | |
| ZEYE COTEN M. | 16.9.17 | | " D.A.C. | |
| | 17.9.17 | | Inspected 187 Bgde A.C. | |
| | 18.9.17 | | Inspected 218, 33, 04, 231 Companies R.E. and 19th M.V. Sn. Pigeoniers | |
| | 20.9.17 | | Conference of Veterinary Officers | |
| | 21.9.17 | | Dispatch p. No. 1 Army Veterinary Training Conference at X Corps ABEELE. | |
| | 22.9.17 | | Visited D.A.C. and 187 Bgde R.A. Inspected 19 Ponies m.v. 61. B. & 4th D.A.C. Office Work 20 CAISTRE | |
| | 23.9.17 | | Office Work 20 CAISTRE | |

# WAR DIARY
## or
## INTELLIGENCE SUMMARY.

Army Form C. 2118.

| Place | Date | Hour | Summary of Events and Information | Remarks and references to Appendices |
|---|---|---|---|---|
| CAISTRE | 24.9.17 | | J.A. Rel: Arrived & Capt. ARMOUR A.K.C. in Relief of Capt JAMES A.K.C. in charge of 190th Brigade R.F.A. D.D. | |
| | 26.9.17 | | Office shifted to LA PANNE. Office very. Section moved to C.39a.2.8. Sheet.19. | |
| LA PANNE | 27.9.17 | | Mobile Vety. Section moved to C.39a.2.8. | |
| | 28.9.17 | | Conference with A.D.V.S. XV Corps. | |
| | 29.9.17 | | Visited 12th Infantry Brigade 190 Field Ambulance 237 Coy R.E. and 238 Machine Gun Company. Mobile Vety. Section moved to Bray DUNES D1a.2.8. | |
| | 30.9.17 | | Brown 98d advance Party for Dressing Cover at NEW ZEALAND CAMP, COXYDE. | |

W B Gilles
D.A.D.V.S.

Vol 18 War Diaries
for October 1917
C.W.B. Sykes. Major A.V.C
D.A.D.V.S. 61st Division
and
O.C. 52nd Mobile Veterinary Section

**Army Form C. 2118.**

# WAR DIARY
or
## INTELLIGENCE SUMMARY.
(Erase heading not required.)

Instructions regarding War Diaries and Intelligence Summaries are contained in F. S. Regs., Part II. and the Staff Manual respectively. Title pages will be prepared in manuscript.

| Place | Date | Hour | Summary of Events and Information | Remarks and references to Appendices |
|---|---|---|---|---|
| LA PANNE | 2.10.19 | | W. J. Street. Visit St. IDESBALDE Railhead to examine lines | |
| | 3.10.19 | | Organised 124 Infantry Brigade at GHYVELDE | |
| | 4.10.19 | | Capt F.K. PERRY A.V.C. evacuates sick Mule Veterinary Section | |
| | 5.10.19 | | Visited COXYDE to arrange for Mobile Veterinary Section | |
| | 6.10.19 | | Organised 122 Infantry Brigade at LA PANNE | |
| | 7.10.19 | | Attended Conference at XV Corps | |
| | | | E Buck transferred to St. IDESBALDE | |
| | | | R.Bijo Veterinary Section moved to St. IDESBALDE | |
| | | | at No. 11 C.C.S. April 11. | |
| S. IDESBALDE | 8.10.19 | | Organised 124th of Infantry Brigade | |
| | | | Arranged Stable for Jobbing horses at COXYDE | |
| | | | BAINS at X.I.C 9,8,5 Nos 6. | |
| | | | 9, remounting horses at St. IDESBALDE Railhead | |
| | 9.10.19 | | Opening of D Veterinary Stable | |
| | | | Inspected 68th K.R.R. Regt. and 13th HANTS at BRAY DUNES | |
| | 10.10.19 | | Inspected 18 Y Brigade R.F.A. at GHYVELDE | |

# WAR DIARY
## or
## INTELLIGENCE SUMMARY.
*(Erase heading not required.)*

Army Form C. 2118.

| Place | Date | Hour | Summary of Events and Information | Remarks and references to Appendices |
|---|---|---|---|---|
| ST IDESBALDE | 11.10.17 | | Visited 128 Infantry Brigade | |
| | 13.10.17 | | Attended Conference at X Corps. Division Conference at D.H.Q. Discussed Remounts at Divisional Trains & Registers | |
| | 14.10.17 | | Visited 181 Brigade R.F.A. at LA PANNE. Attended Shoot of 6" COXYDE BAINS Siege Battery in duty form | |
| | 15.10.17 | | Capt. J.F. WILLIAMS A.V.C. reported for duty. No. 6.2.8 Veterinary Hospital at B. ECHELON. D+G. Inspected Remounts Evacuated horses. Visited N° 1 DESBALDE Culvert & COXYDE BAINS | |
| | 16.10.17 | | Attended Shoot of 19 Siege Battery R.F.A. | |
| | 17.10.17 | | Inspection of Infantry Stables. Visited 164 Howitzer R.F.A. | |
| | 18.10.17 | | Enquiries of Veterinary Officers R.F.A. and Infantry Staff. | |
| | 19.10.17 | | Visited 187 Brigade R.F.A. | |

# WAR DIARY or INTELLIGENCE SUMMARY

| Place | Date | Hour | Summary of Events and Information | Remarks and references to Appendices |
|---|---|---|---|---|
| ST IDESBALDE | 20.10.17 | | 2nd in command at X.X. Corps. Visited 16th Bde RFA. | |
| | 21.10.17 | | Attended Bty Cmdrs Conference at D.H.Q. Visited 16th Bde R.F.A. Granted 10 days leave to ENGLAND | |
| | 22.10.17 | | Coy A.C.S. Visited 19th A.C.S. and country Bde of 2nd Bde | |
| | 23.10.17 | | Visited H/188 and country Bde of 2nd Bde | |
| | 24.10.17 | | Visited 122 Bde RFA, & visited Trans. Inspected 187 Bde RFA. and 133 ady artry | |
| | 25.10.17 | | Visited 188 Bde RFA. Conference at Veterinary Staff | |
| | 26.10.17 | | Visited 187 Bde and RFA & Infantry Staff. | |
| | 27.10.17 | | Conference at X.X. Corps. 6 Coxyde Bains. | |
| | 28.10.17 | | Basil Dulcintrit by Infantry with Ch. | |
| | 29.10.17 | | 19 Bde travel to MALO LES BAINS. | |

# WAR DIARY or INTELLIGENCE SUMMARY
(Army Form C. 2118.)

| Place | Date | Hour | Summary of Events and Information | Remarks and references to Appendices |
|---|---|---|---|---|
| MALO LES BAINS | 30.10.17 | | Visited 187 Brigade R.F.A @ HYVELDE, Inspected Kit & Linseed Impregnated by Smell Fire Mobile Veterinary Section loaned to PONSDITE Mobile Veterinary Section a/c 28 a.i.8. Section 9. Farm Mobile Veterinary Section. | |
| | 31.10.17 | | Tested | |

J. W. O. Ab Mgr
Major
D.A.D.V.S.